D1452661

ONE DESTINY

BOOKS BY SHOLEM ASCH

SHOLEM ASCH

One Destiny

AN EPISTLE
TO THE CHRISTIANS

TRANSLATED BY MILTON HINDUS

G. P. PUTNAM'S SONS

New York

MANUFACTURED IN THE UNITED STATES OF AMERICA

THEN I said, I will not make mention of him, nor speak any more in his name. But his word was in mine heart as a burning fire shut up in my bones, and I was weary with forbearing, and I could not stay.

JEREMIAH 20: 9

Contents

ONE DESTINY

Chapter I

BY THE WILL OF GOD

IN the young manhood of our people when it was imbued with lusty shepherd strength, our fathers, rocking in the humps of their camels across the desert, saw the stars in the sky. The stars became transparent windows, and they saw the Almighty of all the universe, and they fell on their faces before Him, stretched out their hands to Him and cried, "Thou art our God!"

From that time on, my people holds fast to the vision of one living God over all the worlds and over the whole of humanity, Who alone is worthy of being praised and sanctified, Who alone is capable of giving salvation, and through Whom alone man becomes the lord of creation. Through Him alone man raises himself above a worm's fate. He becomes the conqueror of his animal nature; he steps across the narrow limitations of his allotted span of years and becomes a part of heaven, higher than an angel, with his feet planted firmly on the earth and his head in the clouds. He has extended his earthly days, has spun a net to arrest his fall—and, behold! nothing can happen to him any more; he belongs to God; from Him he has come and to Him he returns, deathless, immortal, a veritable heir of eternity.

The talisman of salvation, the saving grace which our

fathers have passed into our hands, was appointed not for our-selves alone but for all people and for the whole world. The God Whom they beheld was the God Who had created heaven and earth. He is the God of Genesis, of the beginning of time. He is the Lord of the world because He created the world and all that it contains. He is the God of all people, of all nations, because He is the One Who created the father of all people, the prototype of humanity, Adam himself.

Only such a god could have had a real existence and sur-vived, because without these attributes, the same fate would have overtaken the God of Israel as overtook the gods of Ammon, Moab, of Moloch and Ashdod.

The favor made manifest by God to our father Abraham was meant not only for his children and his children's chil-dren. God spread His benevolence over all people and made our father Abraham the father of many nations—"In thy seed shall all the nations of the earth be blessed."

The vision of an omnipotent God for all people, though this deity makes a covenant with only one tribe, was steadily before Abraham's eyes from the beginning. It was born to-gether with the creation of the Jews, is kneaded into the very embryo of the Jewish faith; without it, our beginning would not have been from the Creation and our derivation would not have been from Adam, but our beginning and our deriva-tion would have been from Abraham.

The Jewish faith did not develop from a family to a tribal one, from a tribal to a world faith, but had pretended from its earliest beginnings to be the only and all-encompassing one. That is why the Jewish God is such a jealous God. He does not tolerate and will not admit any other deity besides Himself. He is the One and Only, the Sole-Existing, and everything else is idolatry, impurity, and vice. Forbidding the existence of another godhead next to Himself implies perforce the all-embracing character of the Jewish God.

A little less than two thousand years ago, there came into our world among the Jewish people and to it a personage who gave substance to the illusion perceived by our fathers in their dream. Just as water fills up the hollowness of the ocean, so did he fill the empty world with the spirit of the one living God. No one before him and no one after him has bound our world with the fetters of law, of justice, and of love, and brought it to the feet of the one living Almighty God as effectively as did this personage who came to an Israelite house in Nazareth in Galilee—and this he did, not by the might of the sword, of fire and steel, like the lawgivers of other nations, but by the power of his mighty spirit and of his teachings. He, as no one else before him, raised our world from "the void and nothingness" in which it kept losing its way and bound it with strong ties of faith to the known goal, the predetermined commandment of an almighty throne so as to become a part of the great, complete, everlasting scheme of things. He, as no other, raised man from his probationary state as a beast, from his dumb, blind, and senseless existence, gave him a goal and a purpose and made him a part of the divine. He, as no other, works in the human consciousness like a second, higher nature and leaves man no rest in his animal state, wakens him, calls him, raises him, and inspires him to the noblest deeds and sacrifices. He, as no other, stands before our eyes as an example and a warning—both in his divine form and in his human one—and demands of us, harries us, prods us to follow his example and carry out his teachings. Through his heroic life, he casts us down like dust before his feet. No one but he sheds about himself such an aura of moral power, which, with a divine touch, has molded our world and our character; and no one's strength but his own has reached into our time, being the most potent influence in our everyday lives, inspiring us to goodness and exalted things, being the measure and scale for our deeds at every hour and every minute.

Many of us who, for one reason or another, are unable to believe in or whose religious nature cannot conceive of—the physical resurrection of Jesus of Nazareth on the third day after his crucifixion, as the Christian faith teaches, must nevertheless admit, unless the outrages of the church have struck them blind, that in a moral and spiritual sense the Nazarene rises from the dead every day, every hour, and every minute in the hearts of millions of his believers.

If Jesus was not actually restored to life three days after his burial, then he was resurrected every day, every hour, and every minute in the first three hundred years after his death. What must remain an eternal mystery to those who are blind and deaf enough not to believe in miracles is the spread of Christianity during the first three hundred years. No intellectual evidence, no rationalistic explanation can clarify the phenomenon or see it as anything other than an extraordinary development which remains outside the bounds of our intellectual, sensible point of view. Every statement of historians and philosophers falls out of the intellectual frame into which the learned historians have wanted to cram the phenomenon. There was not enough reason for the pagan world to violate its own nature and to stifle its *Zeitgeist* with what was—for it—so foreign, so unrealizable, so antagonistic, so Asiatic a faith. If the Nazarene was revolutionary in blazing a new path for the Jewish spirit, then his teachings, his essence, were not only incomprehensible to the Graeco-Roman spirit but were the opposite of everything which it considered to be the mission and the purpose of humankind. If the pagan peoples suffered from the need of a change in religion, they could have found enough material for it within their own spiritual realm. It was possible, within the framework of their own customs, thoughts, and conduct to work out a religious ethic through the teachings of the Neo-Platonists and the Stoics. And surely it is childish and naïve to explain the phenomenon by the fact that the apostles of the new faith made its acceptance easier for the pagans through making compromises with the old Jewish law. In face of the danger in which the pagan placed his very existence, what effect could it have had if he imbibed the new belief with milk, as the apostle expresses it, or with vinegar? What attraction could the compromise with Jewish law have had for him when acceptance of the belief—with or without compromises—made the newly converted Christian a candidate for the distinction of being thrown to the beasts in the arena?

Naturally we label as "wonders" the occurrences which we cannot explain or of which we are unable to find the actuating causes. The lack of cause is not very often evident in the case of those events which we witness in our lifetime. Wonders are not always created instantly. I should say that miracles become distinct only after an interval of years has elapsed. For often wonders conceal themselves within a veil of natural events, a line of happenings which drag out over a long period.

We can explain with the aid of our intelligence the details of these events as they unfold, linked together in a chain of causes. Often we ourselves are carried along by the events, like dust and straw through storm and wind, and we can't see them, can't realize them, because we are involved in the howl of the storm. Only when the happenings separate themselves off from us and we are able to contemplate them objectively across a historical distance, freed from the wings of the storm that bore us, are we frightened by the misty halo which encircles them, by the transcendent mystery and incomprehensibleness of their appearance, and by the divine radiance which emanates from them. A heavenly blessing, an ununderstandable charm, which sheds from itself the veils and wrappings of real events, separates itself from the gray, everyday, understandable happenings, and remains before our eyes in its entire wonderful transcendence. It separates itself from the dreary, everyday happenings of history and stands out, marked with the incomprehensible, mystic sign which we call wonder.

Perhaps such historical wonders happen and have happened at the establishment of every other faith or every other people. I, as a Jew, whose every move is bound up with the God of Israel, want to know nothing of any other historical wonder, of any other faith, save only the wonder and the faith which radiate from the God of Israel. The wonder is revealed to me in two ways: first, the miracle of the preservation of Israel, second, the miracle of the spread of the Judaeo-Christian idea in the pagan world. The whole thing to me represents a single, divine event. I see in both phenomena the single will of the God of Israel. Not only because I consider my Christian brothers as the spiritual children of Abraham, Isaac, and Jacob, entitled together with me to our birthright from God, but also because I see in pure Christianity an entirely justified share of faith in the God of Israel—through the Messianic idea—equal to my own Jewish faith. The preservation of Israel and the preservation of the Nazarene are one phenomenon. They depend on each other. The stream must run dry when the spring becomes clogged, and Christianity would become petrified if the Jews, God forbid, should cease to exist. And just as the spring loses its value, becomes spoiled and moldy when it has lost its mission and does not water the stream, so would Jewry itself become petrified, barren, and dry if there were no Christendom to fructify it. Without Christendom, Jews would become a second tribe of Samaritans. The two are one. And notwithstanding the heritage of blood and fire which passionate enmity has brought between them, they are two parts of a single whole, two poles of the world which are always drawn to each other, and no deliverance, no peace, and no salvation can come until the two halves are joined together and become one part of God.

Whoever works, strives, and desires that this may come to pass is on the side of God. Whoever does otherwise belongs to the other party.

This is my spiritual credo. On this foundation I have built my house. For this I have sacrificed everything. This faith is my spiritual ego, my physical and spiritual personality. With it I stand and with it I fall.

That is why, as a Jew, as an "outsider," I claim the right to call you my brothers, believers in the Messiah, and, as brothers, to talk with you openly and freely. As children who have the same parents, children of Abraham, Isaac, and Jacob, Christians, Jews, believers in the Messiah, give me your attention, because a brother speaks to you in the name of millions of your brothers.

Chapter II

IN THE SHADOW OF DEATH

IN the dining car of the reserved train that runs from Berlin to Warsaw—a special train for high-ranking military men and government functionaries of the German Reich—there sat an extraordinarily high official whose sudden appearance in the car had evoked tense attention from the military men and dignitaries seated comfortably around the table that was being served. The official himself, whose modesty and friendliness were well known, did everything both by his unobtrusive behavior and his amiable smiles (which were painstakingly forced from his nearsighted eyes and small mouth) to bring his companions back into the easy humor in which he had found them on entering the car. He did not succeed, however.

His position as chief of the Gestapo, his reputation as a pitiless, bloodthirsty, cruel man, his close ties with the Führer—all this kept not only the military men but even his retinue, his aides who accompanied him everywhere and formed a guard to protect him, in an attitude of alert watchfulness. Under the pressure of fear which his personality radiated from itself, the orderlies served the food with trembling hands, which communicated the nervous tension from the waiters to the guests.

The high official, dining very sociably, kept entertaining his staff, which consisted entirely of high-ranking Gestapo men, with anecdotes about the life and behavior of his neighbors, the farmers and rustics around his estate in Bavaria. All people knew that the great man was a farmer in private life. He loved to raise chickens, and tended to his garden himself. In the evenings he would visit the local inn to while away the time over a mug of beer or a game of dominoes.

Here, too, in the midst of very highly placed military men, he ignores this or that general with whom he does not happen to be on good terms, and strives to ingratiate himself with the functionaries or even ordinary civilians—merchants, manufacturers, representatives of great industrialists—who are traveling east to ransack the rich land there (Poland, the Ukraine) and to milk it dry on behalf of the Reich, to enslave it as they have already enslaved the people born on the land, the people of the east.

The Reich is standing on the topmost peak of military ascendancy in the whole world. It is in the early spring of the year which we count as nineteen hundred and forty-two after the birth of the founder of the Christian faith. Never before has a program of world conquest, set for itself by a great power and openly proclaimed, been carried out with such lightning military speed as the German world conquest proclaimed by Adolf Hitler. It looks very much as if our earth, because of this or that transgression, is being put away from the care of God and given over entirely to the power of the destroyer, who has achieved his ends not through human power but with the aid of an infernal strength, which Satan has placed at his disposal.

Military triumphs have made the world a field ready for the new order which Hitler proclaimed in *Mein Kampf*. The German armies stand at the gates of Moscow, and the whole area from the Volga to the English Channel, from the northern rocks by the Norwegian fjords to the Egyptian pyramids, lies raped before the feet of the destroyer. The rest of our miserable world stands silent with bated breath and trembling knees, filled with the feverish panic which the diabolical power summons up in it.

Even in the camp of those who muster their remaining strength to fight against him, loud betraying cries are heard for subservience to the devil because the power belongs to him and not to God.

Strong and mighty as a god—and that is how he is openly acclaimed by his apostles—Hitler begins with an iron hand, with blood-and-thunder, to carry out the program of his new order, the order of a higher master race.

France lies trampled at his feet. Her sons are sent away in guarded trains to the industrial prisons of Germany. Her fields must supply the necessary wine, fruit, and oil.

Norway and Holland are permitted to supply mixing material for the superior German race. The strongest women and girls are picked, and they are paired with German youth.

The Slavs are designated by the Führer's order as inferior races which were created to be eternal slaves. They are not entitled to the privileges of education; they are destined to be *robotniks* (workers) for the *Herrenvolk*. To carry this out, Hitler, the god, has appointed his first apostle, the inventor and founder of the race myth, Dr. Rosenberg, to be ruler over the conquered Slavic peoples. Captured soldiers of the Russian armies are not dealt with according to the accepted conventions for the treatment of prisoners: Instead they are transformed, along with the whole population of the conquered countries, into robotniks, into slave legions which are to serve German agricultural economy and domestic needs.

The Jewish people, which is made responsible for the old order of Christian civilization, is likely to awaken and prod the conscience of the world against the dominion of the new god. It carries within itself the destructive seeds of a Jewish-Christian idea which made the German race an underling of their god Christ—the Jewish race is a danger to the existence of the new order and must therefore be entirely obliterated.

The resolution and the power to execute this sentence upon a whole people is carried now by the chief of the Gestapo—Himmler—in a dreadful document, which is in his brief case. He keeps the brief case near him. His hairy hand rests on it all the time. He doesn't take his eyes off it.

That night the high official slept peacefully on the train between Berlin and Warsaw, with the document in the brief case beside him.

On the second day, Gestapo Chief Himmler in the company of his official retinue rode through the crowded streets of the Warsaw Jewish ghetto to examine it before its destruction.

What did the Gestapo Chief see?

That which was called the Warsaw ghetto was concentrated in the poorest, most overpopulated Jewish quarter. In this area, during the years before the war, lived a population of barely seventy thousand souls. Into that quarter were driven Jews from foreign countries—from Germany, from France, from Holland, and from other occupied territories. The population of the Warsaw ghetto contained now, according to official figures, upwards of five hundred and fifty thousand human beings. People who had spent their whole lives under civilized, European conditions—some of them brought up in luxury and ease—were driven out overnight from the homes, which they or their fathers had built, from their cities and countries to which they had belonged for hundreds of years and scores of generations, were transported under the most inhuman conditions to Poland and thrown into the Dantean hell which was called "the Warsaw ghetto."

The Angel of Death and his messengers, the epidemic illnesses, cut a full slice of destruction there. The mortality rate in the ghetto increased, standing at more than double the death toll among the Warsaw population in the other parts of the city.

The German Gestapo kept constant watch over the open maw of the god Moloch—into which the ghetto had become transformed—supplying ever new victims: men, women, and children taken from the cities of Europe, from Berlin, Frankfort, Darmstadt, Amsterdam, Brussels, Paris—the Jewish citizens of all these cities.

At that time, in the Warsaw ghetto, more than twenty souls lived in a single room which in normal times, even in this overcrowded, never very clean quarter, would have accommodated only one and two.

The ghetto was cut off and isolated by a thick wall from

the poorest streets of the city of Warsaw. German police and Gestapo men, armed with rifles and machine guns, guarded the wall. To leave the ghetto without permission meant to be shot without trial. The population, thrown together into this bed of Sodom, lost every outward sign of civilized living. Clothes became worn out, underwear was infested with lice, shoes were torn.

A small portion, healthy young people whom the Germans used in their war industry, got skimpy rations—just enough to sustain the soul. The rest of the population—the old, the women, the children—were sentenced to a slow death of starvation.

The nights were bereft of all human intercourse by the shutting down of the electric lighting system. The inhabitants of the ghetto froze in the dark during the long winter nights because the fuel supply was also cut off from them.

All education for children and grownups was forbidden; all social life and its pastimes were strictly interdicted.

And yet the ghetto went on, organized itself, and continued to spin the thread of life, which even the sharp German sword was not able to cut. If one was unable to live in freedom, in God's shining sun, then one crept under the earth. In the labyrinthine corridors of the old houses, work continued, a fruitful cultural activity which could only be carried out by a people that had survived the Middle Ages, the persecutions and sufferings with which Jewish history is so amply filled; a people that is destined by the Almighty to live forever.

The Jewish student youth gathered the children together. In the courtyards, among ash cans and privies, war gardens had been planted, and there, in spite of the Gestapo, regular classes for the children were conducted.

In the darkened rooms, cut off from electric light, evening courses were given for adults.

Musical concerts were held which ghetto artists gave for their ghetto brothers. Lectures by learned men and writers were read on broadly branching scientific and literary themes. A regular technical school was conducted with advanced courses given by experienced teachers and savants.

But not only did the ghetto organize itself in the cultural domain where it carried on its private battle in the dark with the destroyer of the world. It did so, too, in the economic and domestic realms. In secret bakeries Jewish bakers baked bread out of white flour smuggled into the ghetto; often the flour came from the German Gestapo, which sold it dearly to the Jews. A committee in the Jewish community saw to it that the bread reached the hungry mouths free of charge, free to those who needed it.

Jewish women stood in secret community kitchens, and with their accustomed skill, with family sorcery which they inherited from their mothers, cooked meals of grits and soups composed of nonexistent materials. Other women and old men sat in attics or cellars and sewed and patched old clothes. Whether it was a wedding dress once laid away in a Jewish household, or a grandfather's worn-out sheepskin extracted piecemeal from a flour or a potato sack—everything was used over again and sewed up into clothes to cover the nakedness of women and children. Others, out of the old shoes, out of leather goods, out of pieces of rubber picked up in odd corners, made shoes and patches to cover the barefoot.

Whole detachments of youths, with iron rods and sticks, transformed into gardens each ruined heap which was all that remained of the houses of the ghetto after the German cannon and bombs had done with them. Others formed sanitary brigades, and these, with the scanty utensils that the Germans left them, cleaned the refuse cans and the outhouses of the ghetto yards, kept order in the corridors and overcrowded houses and rooms.

That is how the Warsaw ghetto, under the heel of the German boot, organized its will to live through its talent for endurance and resistance.

And meanwhile death did its work. There was a contest between the Angel of Death and the Gestapo commissar of the ghetto as to which could surpass the other. Death kept cutting and destroying the Jewish population—old men, women, children—and the German commissar helped it by supplying ever new victims. As soon as a corner of the Warsaw ghetto became empty because of the death of people, whom the inhabitants carried out into the street at night, the commissar was ready to supply ten other Jews, brought from the occupied lands, to take the place of the dead and to become themselves candidates for death.

The Warsaw ghetto became transformed into a slaughterhouse, through which there passed the whole Jewish population of Europe, from the most prominent Jewish families down, from the best-known Jewish firms, names which resounded throughout the world and brought honor and praise to their countries by their accomplishments in every realm of human culture.

The ghetto became the whirlpool into which the Nazi

power sank the European Jewish population and those who were descended from Jews. It became the courtyard of death into which Hitler drove all the non-Aryans of Europe.

When Himmler and his retinue, in strongly armored cars, made their early morning inspection tour through the streets of the ghetto, they noticed, among the sick children who were playing there with the living corpses, also the dead corpses, which had been ejected, stark naked and covered only with papers, from the houses of the ghetto. But this was not enough for the German power—the Jews were not dying fast enough; so the Nazis overtook the Angel of Death and left him behind.

It was always Hitler's method to attract the local population through his agents, to make them partners to his looting, murderous deeds, and to drag them into the swamp of sin and murder into which he had dragged the whole German people along with him.

This time, too, Hitler's Gestapo chief created a motto for the Polish population, a battle cry for his intended plan. On placards in the Warsaw streets, in the newspapers which the Gestapo controlled, there appeared a watchword:

"One mouth less of theirs, one loaf more for us."

That meant that the slaughter of the Jews in Poland was being done in the interests of the Polish people.

It was in the year five thousand seven hundred and five, according to the Jewish reckoning, or the year nineteen hundred and forty-two after the birth of the founder of Christianity, to which Germany, as a part of the civilized world, had been committed for a period of over a thousand years. On the ninth day of Ab, on the day prepared by God for the punishment of the Jews—the day on which the Holy Temple made of stone was twice destroyed—on that day in our time the living Holy Temple of Jewish flesh and blood was once more annihilated. In our days, too, a biblical slaughter of children was found necessary. Streets and sections of the ghetto were surrounded by Gentiles, agents of the Nazi police, in the company of Lithuanian and some Ukrainian elements which had gone over to the service of the Germans. The houses were cut off from all traffic with the street, so that escape or concealment was impossible, and the chase after the children began. Infants were literally torn from their mothers' arms, taken from the breast, thrown into vans and wagons which waited in front of the houses, driven away to the Otvotsk railroad or Muranov Place, packed into locked freight cars, and taken to the execution centers, which had been prepared earlier for the purpose with gas and smoke chambers, in the woods of Treblinka and Bielzshets.

Of course, the mothers did not give away their children easily. There began a life-and-death struggle with the frantic women. Many a mother had to be killed before she would allow her arms to be wrenched from her child. Others threw themselves down with their infants from the upper stories into the street to find death together with their sucklings. No knout, no bayonet, no bullet helped. Mothers fought with bare hands against swords and guns. But their efforts were in vain.

Within a short time, all children ranging in age from a day to sixteen years were liquidated in the Warsaw ghetto. All children in special homes, orphan asylums, sanitariums were taken out to be exterminated together with the teachers and the guardians who brought them up.

Smuggling and trading in children's lives became a thriving industry. For a large sum of money it was possible to smuggle a child out of the ghetto and to hide it in a Polish Christian house. It was true that such an act invited death, but volunteers were to be found, among the Polish population on the other side of the wall, who were willing for a sum of forty to fifty thousand zlotys—that is, from ten to twelve thousand dollars— to risk their lives by concealing a child that was smuggled out. The "luxury" of saving the children from the frying chambers of Treblinka and Bielzshets could be afforded only by the very rich who had been able to conceal such sums from the Gestapo men. But these children, too, were not destined to live long. The sum had hardly been paid when the child was thrown out on the streets of Warsaw—a fate which meant certain death.

There were cases, too, when the Christian foster father, after getting the money, wanted to rid himself of the shadow hanging over him and turned the child over to the Gestapo. Whatever the case, few parents succeeded in saving their children. These few were among the very wealthy who could afford to pay the ransom. For the poor, there was no salvation, no escape.

Still, there were some isolated cases of Christian conduct among the Polish people. Because of this, a desperate child occasionally succeeded in escaping the ring of death. Sometimes a youngster dared to climb over the high barbed-wire wall of the ghetto, or found some other means, which only a child strengthened by his youthful will to live could have found.

Such children who managed to smuggle themselves through the lethal ring flitted like shadows into the dark hallways of Polish dwellings and knocked with deadly fear upon strange doors. In most cases they were turned away by Poles who were frightened for their own lives, but in some instances a human hand reached out and took them in and treated them according to the commandments of their faith or quite simply those of human feelings alone, in spite of the risks which this involved.

The most Christian deeds are recorded among the Catholic clergy and among the sisters of various orders. Escaped children, driven by their instinct for survival, sought protection and support under the roofs of God's dwellings, in churches and in cloisters. The subsequent fate of these children is unknown. Gratitude and recognition ought to be expressed here, however, to the scattered souls who bore witness through their deeds to the truth of their faith in Christianity's hour of greatest need and trial.

The extirpation of the children of the Warsaw ghetto merely served as a stimulant for the blood lust of the Nazi brutes. Moloch opened wide his mouth and cried, "More! More!"

Whole detachments of Nazi soldiery, reinforced by Finnish, Lithuanian, and Ukrainian elements (the Lord be praised for saving the Polish people from the fatal stigma which others impressed upon the memory of their nations for the remainder of human history), began to drive together the Jewish population of the Warsaw ghetto from the houses into the streets, where were waiting the identical vans, the boards and floors of which were still covered with the congealed blood of their children. They were put into the wagons or driven on foot—whole crowds of old Jews, women, and girls. Invalids were dragged from their beds, and those who could not leave were murdered on the spot.

Hemmed in by a ring of death with bayonets and rifles, battalions of people dragged themselves across the streets of the ghetto, singing, praying, crying out to God with the same prayers which accompanied victims in former days on their way to the stakes of the Inquisition, the same outcry heard on the cross from him who gave his life to save the world, *"Eli, Eli, lama sabachtani?"*—"My God, my God, why hast thou forsaken me?" That same cry was heard on the streets of Warsaw from hundreds of souls who, with their crosses, were being whipped on the way to Golgotha.

"Eli, Eli, lama sabachtani?"—with this difference, that the cry on Golgotha was heard in the company of the swords and spears of Roman idolators, while the cry on the Warsaw streets sounded among clubs and bayonets of people who had been converted, who called themselves Christian folk.

"Ropes of death have encompassed me, and toils of the pit have overtaken me. I meet with trouble and sorrow. I then called on the name of the Lord. I pray thee, Lord, release my soul."

"My tears have become my bread by day and night as they say to the whole time: Where is thy God?"

And the answer which the Christian martyrs once made to themselves as they waited for death in the cellars of the Roman arenas, a death which they heard in the roaring of the lions—that same answer and consolation were now given by the Jews one to another as they joined hands together.

"Why art thou bowed down, my soul, and why must thou murmur within me? Trust in the Lord, for I will praise Him, my supporter and my God."

"Whither shall I turn from Thy spirit? And where shall I find escape from before Thy countenance?"

And a Chassid called out the answer in a joyful voice, just as if he were in his rabbi's house:

"I shall pass before my Lord in the lands of the living."

In the death trains which stretched from the streets of the ghetto to the places of execution were all kinds of Jews. There were Jews who, from birth, had not known that they were Jews, whom Hitler instructed in the Judaism in which their parents had failed to instruct them. They did not know or understand the meaning of their life, still less the meaning of their death. There were Jews from Germany, apostates or half-apostates, Jews who had reckoned themselves Germans throughout their existence. Many of them considered themselves Aryan and campaigned within the very ghetto walls for the recognition of their Aryan status by the Gestapo. They looked upon their Jewishness as a mistake, as an oversight on the part of authority. There were Jews from Amsterdam and Antwerp who thought themselves Hollanders and Belgians respectively. The Jews of Poland itself were likewise divided, fragmented, many of them assimilated for generations, others who had been converted and looked upon themselves as Catholics. Notwithstanding these differences, all of them were thrown into the same pot with the devout, Chassidic, Polish Jews of Warsaw. Many of them suddenly found themselves. The voice of blood made itself heard in their veins during their death march across the ghetto.

The blood of their heritage—Sinai, acceptance of the Torah, Moses, Joshua, Amos, the sages of the Mishnah, the rabbis, the generations of holy men, martyrs through the whole length of bloody history—awoke, sprang up alive out of the ashes of their superficial assimilation. They sang together with the rest, cried, called out the chapters of the Psalms, which seemed almost as if they were created directly through the blood heritage of their fathers, flowing through their veins. They destroyed the artificial boundaries, made nothing of partitions, and now an assimilated German Jew, the discipline of whose Prussian military upbringing is still evident in his posture and in his walk, holds on, literally hangs on the arm of a bedraggled, Polish, Chassidic Jew. Holding hands together are a Frankfort patrician and a Polish Chassidic pauper, a French advocate and a Jewish peddler of starch, an Antwerp diamond merchant and a German professor from Berlin, all together with a baggage carrier from Warsaw, a musician from Vienna, a convert next to a Chassid, a Parisian lady next to a Jewish woman from the poorest neighborhood, a female storekeeper arm in arm with the wife of a Dutch senator, an apostate with cross in hand next to a rabbi who presses his Taluth and phylacteries to his heart—wants to die in his prayer shawl. A former apostate holds the hand of a cantor, presses himself toward the group of rabbis with long surcoats and ear-curls, who cry out and call aloud the verses of the Psalms, which have accompanied Jews to all the hecatombs, the *autos-da-fé,* in every crisis and every slaughter they have suffered for their faith throughout the ages.

"Yea, though I walk through the valley of the shadow of death, I shall fear no evil, for Thou art with me."

The unlettered as well as the learned understand the words (spoken in Hebrew), not from mouth to ear but through blood and vein. It is the voice of blood which talks, it is the song of Jewish faith which sings in the Jew's blood.

And suddenly everything becomes understandable, realizable, clear, and beautiful. Suffering acquires a reason, an explanation—it is the highest price exacted for one's faith. The Jew from Paris, Amsterdam, Antwerp, Berlin, Frankfort, becomes simply a Jew. The Jewish Aryans, the Jews who are half-Aryans but want to become whole ones, have disappeared; there are no longer any converted Jews or nearly converted Jews; there are no longer nationalist or assimilated Jews, no longer Jewish bolsheviks, Bundists, or Zionists; no longer religious or irreligious Jews. There is only one kind of Jew—the plain, unadorned Jew, the Jew of the Psalms, the son of Abraham, Isaac, and Jacob, who goes on his eternal way, the way of everlasting Zion, the way of the salvation of Israel.

The prophet Elijah leads the way and makes a path for them. King David is among them, as are the patriarchs and the prophets. And so is the Nazarene.

And so, between the lines of bayonets and guns, shielded only by the divine wings above their heads, they are driven into Muranov Place, to the railroad station, where they are awaited by the unlocked freight cars which are still stained by the dried-up blood of their children. This time, the cars are covered with a thick coat of lime.

They are crowded in like sheep, body to body, head to head, belly to belly. Every boundary of privacy is wiped out. The individual loses his individuality—there is only one living mass of bodies, kneaded one into the other.

The doors of the cars are shut and sealed. The long train filled with human paste departs, stops on a side track, stands for a few days. No water, no air reaches in from the outside. From the cars are heard only—singing cries at first, gurgling cries later on, then heavy sighs, thin voices that can hardly be heard; finally silence.

There stands a long train of sealed cars, packed full of tightly kneaded bodies. When silence settles around the cars, they are taken to the place reserved for human garbage near the slaughterhouses of Treblinka and Bielzshets. Great pits are ready there, dug by other Jews forced to do so, and covered with lime. The cars are conducted by rails to the very edge of the pits.

One car after another rides up and dumps its dead cargo. The bodies are already so completely decomposed by the gases given off by the lime that individuals are no longer recognizable. Those who nevertheless display any signs of life are thrown at once into the gas chambers, which are conveniently at hand.

The cars, emptied of their dead, go back to Warsaw for more corpses.

From the month of July, 1942, up to April, 1943, the trains brought more than half a million souls from the ghetto to the dumping grounds for the dead in Treblinka and Bielzshets, which are stops along the Lublin railroad line. In most cases the Germans were spared the necessity of forcing the prospective corpses into the gas chambers—they had already been burned up by the fumes exuded by the lime in the cars.

In July, 1942, there were 600,000 souls in the Warsaw ghetto;

in April, 1943, about 40,000 were left—young people whom the Germans could keep and use for their war machine.

But one morning when the German police came into the ghetto to take out their daily toll of victims for the gas chambers, they were met by a hail of bullets from broken windows, from roofs, from cracks in doors, from cellar openings. The ghetto assumed an attitude of resistance.

Without any hope of victory or escape, the younger and stronger element, which had for a long time been straining to fight the Germans but had been held back by the older and more pious people, now made up their minds firmly to die a heroic death. And they did die a heroic death. They renewed the tradition of the Maccabeans.

For fifty-six days a handful of Jews, lost, tortured, starved, burned by every fire, armed only with pistols, irons, and cleavers, conducted a bitter battle to the death with the great, awe-inspiring German military machine, which had coped with the whole world. The battle lasted for fifty-six days. Against the mighty heroes of the ghetto, the Germans made use of every instrument and weapon in their arsenal including airplanes and tanks. For fifty-six days the handful of brave men held out against the German beast.

The eagerness to die with honor accomplished wonders. German power found itself incapable of rooting out the handful of heroes. Thousands of Nazi dead fell around the houses of the ghetto.

German prestige began to decline in the eyes of the Polish population. Still, no one came out of the great Polish city to aid in the struggle which the Jews were carrying on against the common foe. Even the few weapons which were supplied by the Polish underground had to be purchased with hard cash.

The Germans were unable to take the ghetto until they resorted to the cowardly expedient of cutting off the water supply, and even then the stronghold of the Warsaw ghetto did not fall as long as the last Jew breathed and could hold a gun in hand.

The six hundred thousand Jews annihilated in the ghetto were only a small fraction of the total number of Jewish victims who fell to the Nazi ax.

The Jews of the Polish provinces were murdered on the spot wherever the Nazi beasts found them. Only the Jews of other countries, of Holland, Belgium, France, Germany, Austria, Norway, were treated ceremoniously and transported to Poland, to the Warsaw ghetto, for destruction.

Hitler and the German war machine must have had good reason, in the crowded conditions of transport during wartime, for bringing the European Jews to Poland before destroying them, instead of doing it out of hand, as they did in Poland. The reason for this was quite simply that the Gestapo bigwigs were afraid of the local populations. The Jews who had dwelt in these places for hundreds and hundreds of years were so closely bound up economically and culturally with the population that, notwithstanding the anti-Semitic agitation which the Hitlerites unloosed in order to prepare the field for the slaughter of the Jews, the populace of the large European cities considered the Jews an integral part of itself. The

Hitlerites, it would have been felt, were destroying not the Jews but the population itself.

And it was feared, too, that the sympathies shown to the suffering Jews by the population even in German cities might be transformed into open demonstrations, a thing that actually happened in many European cities. After the inauguration of the ghetto in Amsterdam, members of the Dutch aristocracy left their homes and went to live with the Jews in the ghetto. In Denmark, upon passage of an edict forcing Jews to wear a yellow patch on their sleeves, the Danish king put on the yellow armband marked with the star of David. Even in Rumania, it is said, in the classic land of anti-Semitism, the "Iron Guard" defended and protected the Jews from the Nazi beast. In Hungary, too, we know that until the very end, when the Nazis took over the government there, the old government, wherever it was not tied up with the Nazis, protected the lives and safety of its eight hundred thousand Jewish citizens, even though they were deprived of means to make a living and robbed of their fortunes. As long as the Hungarian people had even a trace of independence, the Nazi beasts could do nothing against the lives of the Hungarian Jews.

When the Nazi beast desired to destroy the European Jews, therefore, it was forced to transport them to Poland. Whether this was because the Polish population, more than any other, had been corrupted by the disease of anti-Semitism with which the Germans and native-bred Nazis had infected it, and the ground for the atrocities was therefore well prepared; or whether it was because the Poles were not reckoned with at all, being considered not completely human since they were Slavs, the Germans elected to make Poland the slaughter-house of the European Jews.

In my native city of Kutno where Jews had lived for centuries, the Nazis, after capturing the city at the beginning of the war, took the whole Jewish population of over five thousand souls and isolated them in a sugar factory where they were allowed simply to starve to death. They did the same with the Jews of Lithuania, where the local population helped them in their bloody work. In the cities of Latvia and Estonia the first thing the Nazis did when, like a flood, they inundated the Russian provinces with blood and fire, was to massacre the Jewish population. The Jews of the Soviet provinces of Wolin, White Russia, the Ukraine, Krim, the Caucausas, who had lived in peace under the Soviet power after the czarist pogroms and had become an integral part of the general population, employed in all spheres of productive work, were slaughtered by the Nazi brutes, were devoured by the ravenous beast.

In Kiev, in Kharkov, in hundreds of other Ukranian cities, where there had existed a Jewish population of one hundred thousand, an intricately branching group of Jewish activities in every realm of human culture, where Jewish life was teeming, where Jews participated in heavy industry, the Red Armies, when they recaptured the cities, did not find any Jews. It can well be imagined how the Jewish soldiers of the Red Army felt when, in such cities as Kiev, Berdichev, Zhitomir, and Gomel, which for centuries have had a tradition of Jewish life and Jewish scholarship, which had been honored by the Jews with the holy name "Jerusalem" because of their men of learning, their institutions of learning, and their cultural activity—how the Jewish soldiers must have felt when they returned to these cities and found no living Jew in them, only waste places to which the local people pointed and said, "It was here that the brigands buried the ashes of their victims."

Of the fourteen million Jews who were in the world a day before Hitler set fire to it, between eight and nine million lived in the countries overrun by the Nazis. Of these nine million Jews who fell under the sway of the Angel of Death, it is now accepted as fact that about two million were rescued. The largest part of these saved themselves in the land of the Soviets, in the land which, more than any other, was aware of its mission of humanity. The Soviet Union showed the world in deeds how deeply rooted the divine teachings are in the soul of its people, and how false is the accusation spread by the Nazis that the Soviet regime has destroyed the Christian ideal among its people. Quite the contrary, the Soviets during the war demonstrated not only through words but through deeds how deep-rooted was the ideal of the Judaeo-Christian faith. Let that be mentioned to the credit of the Soviet Union. The Jewish people will never forget it.

Nearly a million Jewish souls were saved by the Soviets, snatched from the abyss, from hell; and, in spite of the great shortcomings in her system of transport as a result of the war, the Soviets conveyed them to places of safety, where they dwelt in need together with the rest of the population, but were protected under the wings of a civilized, humane people and a civilized, humane government. It is to be hoped that another million Jews have survived, lost amid the fields, hidden in caves and pits, shielded by the peasant population in occupied territory.

Seven million Jews were devoured by the Nazi beast during the four years of its depredations on the world. Seven million human lives were destroyed by the Nazis not in the heat of battle, not for any military purpose or strategic need, but in order to sate its sadistic, cannibalistic blood lust. The fires of hate which Hitler and the Nazis awakened and nourished in the hearts of the German nation had to be cooled with blood of seven million souls.

Not Hitler alone, not the Gestapo alone, not the Nazis alone, but the whole German people—man, woman, and child —is infected with the leprous plague, the disease of bestiality and blood lust. It had to prey on women and children and old men, had to wallow in human blood, had to smell—like Moloch of old—the odor of human flesh burning.

We do not know what will become of the German people after the war. To plan the physical annihilation of this people is a sin equal to the one the Nazis committed—but the very idea of such a plan is tomfoolery. The German people will live again after the war, will even return someday perhaps to the moral standard set in the days of Goethe and Schiller, before it was infected with the arrogant madness of being a chosen people. Certainly the German people will become again a portion of the civilized world, and we all hope and wish for that time to come quickly, when German genius—and who dares to deny it?—may become as productive for the welfare of humanity as it has been for its destruction. But whatever the fate of the German people as a whole, every German of the forty millions of them—man, woman, and child—will bear the mark of Cain on his forehead forever. And as it was with Cain, so to every German for the remainder of his days on earth the question will be put: "Where is thy brother Abel?" Where are the European Jews? And as the Lord said to Cain, so to every German will be said these words: "What hast thou done? The voice of thy brother's blood cries up to me from the dust."

Because the earth will not cover up the spilt blood of Israel. The whole German people is guilty of the crime which cries out to the heavens. Seven million souls are not annihilated on a single day or by a single hand—the whole people must have given its consent to the monstrous crime or Hitler would not have dared to commit it.

To be sure, the Jews are not Hitler's only victims. I am far from claiming this "distinction" for them. After the Jews, the greatest sufferers perhaps have been the Russians. Hitler acted toward the Russians in about the same way he did toward the Jews. But not only the Jews and the Russians—the whole world, both those who are persecuted directly and those who take their part, is in agony because of German transgression. The groans and outcries of millions upon millions of mothers and children rise to heaven. With no other people, however, did Hitler dare to do what he did with the Jews. When he robbed another people of its freedom, its wealth, when he put tens of millions of free men in chains and set them to work as slaves in his factories, when he transformed whole peoples into inferior races, he still spared their lives. He permitted himself the physical annihilation of the Jewish people only.

For this exception which Hitler made of the Jews, for this choice which he conferred upon them, for the freedom with which he could slaughter a whole people, for this election of the Jews, for this crying sin, the guilt is carried, the accessory guilt if not the full one, by the whole Christian world.

Chapter III

THE POISONED WELL

I HAVE hurled a terrible word. My deepest feelings rebel and protest against this horrible charge. My hands trembled in writing it down. Nights of reconsideration and regret have passed, nights which robbed my eyes of sleep, while I have weighed this accusation. Yet ... whatever the pain and anguish it may bring me, I must let it stay. Because the sin which Hitler, the Nazis, and the whole German people have drawn upon themselves could never have been committed—at any rate, in the measure and form in which it was committed—if it were not inspired, if it were not sanctioned, or at the very least allowed by the criminal silence of a wicked world, shot through with Jew-hatred, with indifference to human wrongs.

Some naïve anti-Semites try mightily to distinguish themselves from the cannibalistic excesses of Hitlerism: We didn't mean it to go so far, they exclaim; we are in favor only of this or that restriction for the Jews; we were only joking. They, as well as the rest of you, are partners in guilt to the Hitlerites and their scandalous deeds. For what Hitler has done is the logical consequence of Jew-hatred, a result of feelings that have been accumulating over many generations. The murders, the strangling of children, the slaughter of women, the burning of old people, the cannibalistic frying and broiling of millions upon millions in gas ovens are a direct result of the exclusion laws, the persecutions, the tortures which have been inflicted upon the Jews by the world. What Hitler has done is merely the crowning point of the anti-Semitic effort.

From the very beginning, Hitler sought a popular victim for his blood lust—a victim whom he might throw to the world as bait in order to entrap it. He wished to pacify the Christian conscience of the world, to put it into a hypnotic trance of hatred and revenge, and so be able to lead it on his leash and do whatever he pleased with it.

He knew just what sort of tune would be sweet to your ears. He tried to satisfy your hatred with the most popular victim, who had been portrayed for generations and generations before your eyes, before your thought and heart, as an outcast of humanity, the enemy, the pariah, the foreigner, the "Jew." Oh, how sweet that melody was which Hitler played in the ears of certain groups, not only the ears of those who are always fishing in troubled waters but of completely innocent, well-meaning, believing Christians, in whom it was possible for Hitler to destroy so easily their belief in God, the teaching of generations, the heritage of human conscience, with the powerful poison which is called anti-Semitism.

Anti-Semitism is not a movement. It is a disease. He who is infected with it is unable to have an orientation, a judgment, or an opinion which is the result of logical thinking or of actual facts. The anti-Semite has no proof, no opinion, no consciousness even, because proof, opinion, and consciousness are attained through independent thought. He has no independent thought, he is imprisoned within the magic circle in which his sufferings have immured him. He has no will of his own. He is ruled by his disease, the name of which is anti-Semitic insanity.

Certainly it is not the intention of the author to deny, to extenuate, or to approve certain characteristic faults of his people, faults which have developed through centuries of accumulated inheritances, a direct result perhaps of the very hatred with which it has been surrounded—faults, or perhaps virtues, which the Jewish people developed because of its isolation. But all this has nothing to do with the matter.

Jews developed their character through thousands and thousands of years under various conditions arising from a multitude of different causes. Belief in salvation, martyrdom, exceptional treatment—all these things have supplied Jewish character with its faults and virtues. As in every other group, the virtues and faults are various—and, therefore, not understandable to others. The qualities change in accordance with the conditions and atmosphere in which the group finds itself. In general, the Jew, because of his rich experience in wandering, is more talented in acclimatizing himself to new places and in accommodating himself to new conditions. Someone has truly said: "Each country has the Jews it deserves." The individual Jew is neither higher nor lower on the scale of moral personality than the individual of any other group.

But anti-Semitism has nothing to do with all this, because anti-Semitism is unable to see, hear, weigh, understand, judge, or analyze events. The anti-Semite is ruled by only one instinct, the instinct of hatred for everything that is not his own.

No one has exposed so clearly the blindness, the lack of judgment, the disease of hatred as did Tertullian, who lived at the end of the second and the beginning of the third century, and who described in his Apology the blind hatred of the Romans for the first Christians.

For the same motive which evokes enmity and suspicion toward the Jews throughout their existence also brought suspicion, hatred, and persecution upon the Christians during the first three hundred years, when they constituted a minority in the Roman world.

What is the basic cause of anti-Semitism? The first and most important reason for hatred of Jews is the separate faith which has isolated them. All other reasons, both economic and political, are a rationalization of this first cause, because the adherence of Jews to a belief different from that of the rest of the population has served to make them regarded throughout all generations as intruders. No matter how long Jews lived in a certain place—they might even have been among the founders of the city, among the earliest builders and inhabitants of it—they were still regarded as foreigners and trespassers, just as they were in Alexandria during the first century.

Because of their separateness or because of persistence in their own faith, the Jews were not recognized as citizens of the cities in which they lived either in Asia or in Greece and had to apply to Caesar for special privileges to safeguard their rights as a minority. Their customs and commandments were derided by every comedian in the circuses and theaters. They were insulted by every lout. The foulest slanders were invented concerning their faith, and they themselves were sometimes physically attacked by the inhabitants when their leaders were unable to protect them. The same thing happened to those elements, both among the Jews and among the heathens, who turned to the new, suspect faith which sprang up in Rome and in the Roman provinces, namely, Christianity.

But it was not only that the slanders and vilifications heaped upon the Jewish faith were carried over to the Christian religion. The Romans with reason regarded Christianity as one branch or form of the Jewish faith—and therefore they poured out upon it the whole flood of suspicion which they had accumulated toward Jewry. Not only did their writers convince the population that the Christians worshiped an ass's head, the same slander which they had spread about the Jewish faith, as Tertullian informs us in his Apology, but they ascribed to the new faith the most bestial horrors, degradation, and inhumanity, which they dared not ascribe even to the Jewish religion because the latter was, after all, recognized by Rome and so was entirely legal.

According to Tertullian, Christians were hated to such an extent in those days that "a Christian, you would have believed, is a man who is guilty of every crime, a foe to the gods, to the emperor, to the law, to morality, a sinner against the laws of nature. . . .

"It is not the man who is guilty of a specific crime; the guilt lies in the name alone. Since 'Christian' is the appellation of an offense, it is not absurd that the offense should lie within the name itself." Are not these words just as well suited to the Jews today?

"There is such general hatred, blind hatred toward the name that everyone who has any mud to throw upon it is readily believed—'Caius Sextus is a good man; a pity that he's a

Christian.' Another says: 'I'm surprised that Lucius Titus who's so bright has suddenly turned Christian.' "

How many times a day does it happen to every one of us to hear the same tune, with this difference only, that the word "Christian" is exchanged in the mouths of Christians for the word "Jew"? And to whom are the words of the Christian apologist of the second century better suited than to the Jews of today?

"Our triumph has both the glory of martyrdom and of eternal life. Though we are annihilated, yet we win the battle. When we are beaten, then are we victorious. In the very mouth of destruction, we are saved.

"Though we are damned by you, we are nevertheless raised and accepted by God."

By whom were these words spoken—by a Christian martyr of the second century, by a rabbi of the Rhine provinces in the time of the Crusades, by an Abarbanel in the time of the Spanish Inquisition, by a chronicler of the Cossack persecutions of the seventeenth century, or by a victim of the Nazis?

"Thou shalt love the stranger, because strangers were ye in the land of Egypt," God instructed us through Moses.

How readily, however, the commandment is forgotten by those who were themselves strangers, as soon as they have become settled inhabitants!

That has been the case of the Christian church.

"I nourished you upon milk like children," the Apostle Paul could say to the Christian converts in Corinth. When the Christians, however, went to spread the tidings to the Jews, they did not "nourish" them upon milk but upon stones. On the point of the sword did they bring to Israel what Paul called "the hope of Israel," and they accomplished the redemption of the tortured Messiah through the fires of the Inquisition. From the day on which Christianity became the ruling group, it brought upon Israel one long night of terror and death.

"I do not wish to record all of the inhumanities practised against us by the Gentiles," writes a chronicler of the days of the Cossack persecutions, "because I do not wish to disgrace the name of man, who was created in the image of God."

"We must pray for our torturers," writes a rabbi of Germany, "because they are the rod with which the Lord chastises us."

One long night of sorrow and pain. The history of the Jews is a bloody sore on the conscience of Christendom.

There was not a single slander invented by the lowest Greek and Roman pamphleteers against the first Christians which the Christians themselves did not later carry over against the Jews and the Jewish faith. How many victims fell, how much Jewish blood was spilled, how much trouble, pain, how many nights of fear, anxiety, terror were caused by the false accusation repeated through century after century that the Jews required human blood for their rituals, an accusation which the Roman pamphleteers had made against the early Christians!

He who would have become the hope of Israel; he who was called upon by God to become the redeemer, promised by God to their fathers; he whom the prophets had foretold as the consolation and reward of all their sufferings and troubles; he who was to have raised Israel to its greatest heights, to become the crown of all their strivings, the light of the world—became instead the source of death and destruction for Israel. "How can we believe that Jesus is the Messiah when he has become the origin of everything evil and wicked that has come over Israel, since his name appeared in the world?" is the painful cry heard in Jewish writings through the centuries. What wonder that the Jews have refused so stubbornly to drink from the well which has contained nothing but poison for them? The responsibility for this lies with those who have contaminated the spring of God with the poison of Satan and of death.

In the drama of the great world event, the coming of the Messiah, in which Israel ought to have occupied a pre-eminent position, the church invented the role of a Judas and an Ahasueras for Israel. And with the aid of its whole powerful authority, with the whole of its strength, the church strove to bestow upon Israel the role she had designated for it. She cut it off from all spheres of productive labor. She crowded, drove, isolated it behind ghetto walls, robbed it of every right and every human freedom—and left it a single path, along which there could evolve only the preconceived type of a Judas or a Wandering Jew. And when the church did not succeed in this, when in the shadow of death, in the crowded streets of the ghetto, in sorrow, in everlasting terror, the Jews nevertheless brought forth great moral spirits and continued to spin the golden thread of Jewish ethics out of Jewish teachings in the spirit of the prophets, this was not with the encouragement and consent of the church but thanks only to the strength of spirit and to the divine springs which God opened in Jewry. The church, on the other hand, continued to issue edicts whose chief purpose was to force upon the Jews the role of the Wandering Jew, and went on driving them from one exile into another.

Is it not an irony, a piece of the devil's wit, that a society which dared to clothe itself with the sacred name of him who is called "the king of the Jews" should set itself the task of becoming the chastising rod for the Jewish people? And the consequence of this was that the name which should have evoked joy and song in the Jewish heart evoked instead deadly anxiety and torturing fear. Jewish blood freezes in one's veins when the blood and tears brought by that name to the Jews are remembered.

From his earliest childhood the Christian is fed upon the milk of hatred toward the people which prepared the creation of his faith and was its very center. The milk of hatred for the Jews is later transformed into blood, a heritage of enmity which has flung its snakelike form from the earliest beginnings of Christianity. The fierce battle which was waged upon the new faith by the hot-blooded Jews at its very inception—a quite natural reaction of every society—has unfortunately left traces of the heated passion found in the writings of both sides at the very beginning. We are suffering for the sins of our fathers. But alongside of the signs of enmity toward the Jews which penetrated into the earliest writings of the church, the New Testament also demonstrates the lofty role played by the Jews as the only people which took upon itself the yoke of heaven. The fact that they were especially chosen is shown to the reader; their heritage is emphasized, the promises of their fathers, the blessings and vows of the prophets, not to mention the words spoken by him who bears the mantle of the Jewish Messiah—he underlined so clearly his role as the Jewish

Messiah—not to mention Saint John or Peter; even Paul, who was the prime cause of the storm, in his Epistle gives to the Jews the most honorable place in the new faith. Not only is the Messiah called "the hope of Israel," but it is indicated there that to Israel belongs the birthright, the promises of the patriarchs, and the legacy. Israel is first in the order of salvation. The Jewish hope, the Jewish longing for deliverance, Israel's whole past, its heritage, its forefathers, its prophets—all this is so closely bound up with faith in the Messiah that the redemption of the Jews becomes practically the first principle of the new faith.

When Jesus the Nazarene appears to his disciples for the first time after the resurrection, the first question which they ask of the Messiah is: "Lord, wilt thou at this time restore again the kingdom to Israel?" So Luke tells us. The restoration of the kingdom of Israel was so important a condition of the messianic faith that the apostles could think of nothing else as the first thing that the Messiah would do when he came back to life but to inaugurate the reign of Israel.

But of all this—of the role of Israel in the new faith, of its honor, of its preparation for the advent of the Messiah, of its place in the messianic hierarchy—nothing whatever is said now, no hint of it is instilled into the hearts of believers. Of the twelve disciples, all Jews, all but one faithful followers of Jesus, only Judas, the unfaithful, became to Christians the symbol of the Jewish people. It would be more fitting to have chosen St. James, the faithful pious Jew, whose Epistle might well have been written by one of the Old Testament prophets. From the beginning the church sought to win adherents not among the Jews but among the Gentiles, among the Greeks and Romans, in order to eradicate the impression, which Roman society correctly had, that the new faith was only a sect, a segment of the religion of the hated Jews.

Since the latter fact was the greatest obstacle to the spread of the new faith, the church began gradually to rid itself of the entire burden of the heritage she had got from the Jews. Jewish holidays were neglected, as were also Jewish customs and Jewish ritual laws which, at the beginning of the religion, had been cardinal items of faith in the Messiah. The days were shifted—the Sabbath was moved from Saturday to Sunday.

I wish in no wise to place the blame for the separation of mother and child upon one side only. That is far from my intention. I am not writing here, however, about the causes of the conflict but merely about the results of the cleavage. If it was easy for the Greek or the Roman to forswear idolatry in going over to the new belief in a Messiah, it was not at all easy for the Jew who stood beneath the eyes of a living God and was enjoined by the Law from the abjuration of his faith. It was not so simple for the Jew to acknowledge a faith in his Messiah which brought nothing but suspicion to him and a mockery of the belief of his fathers. Because the church, from the beginning, in order to attract the Roman and Greek to its fold, not only made compromises with the Mosaic Code —a necessity which is quite understandable—but became more and more estranged from Jewry, denied all connection with it, debased and brought shame upon the Jews. In order to create the impression among the Greek people, who were in the process of being proselytized for the new faith, that Christianity was something entirely separate and had no connection with the Jewish religion, all the blame for the sufferings and death of the founder of Christianity was gradually shifted onto the shoulders of the Jews. Notwithstanding the fact that their Messiah was the Messiah of the Jews, that the fulfillment of Jewish hopes and of Jewish prophecies were ascribed to him, that the Messiah carried all the blessings of Israel, he was nevertheless painted as the victim of Israel. No one but the cursed Jews was to blame for his sufferings and death, which were a necessary condition for his messianic mission. This line of reasoning was pushed to the most extreme limits. Pontius Pilate, the bloody Roman governor who used to make blood baths of the gatherings of pilgrims in the Temple courts during the Jewish holidays, who did not let pass a single opportunity of showing his suspicion of Jewish customs, of Jewish religious institutions over which he had been sent to rule—he, we are told, wanted to spare the Jewish Messiah who both by his name and his mission pretends to the rule of the whole world, which includes, of course, rule over the Jews in place of Caesar, but the Jews in their bloodthirstiness did not permit him. The Roman idolator, Caesar's procurator, has been shown in the act of observing a Jewish ritual on this occasion, a ritual known only among the Jews and finding its origin in the Pentateuch —I refer to the washing of the hands as evidence of innocence in a murder. The water which the church so willingly supplied to Pilate was not clean enough to wash away the bloodstains that were upon his hands, blood of hundreds of thousands of Jewish souls and also of that Jew who is called Jesus the Messiah.

In any case, the legend of the Jewish crucifixion of the savior became the source of limitless, torturing, and senseless

hatred toward the Jews. The legend about the Jewish crucifixion of the Messiah has cost millions of Jewish lives. It
carries a long streak of blood after it, right down to our own
time. It has become the microbe of hate in the spiritual body
of Christianity. It has caused and still causes daily trouble for
the Jews. It brings tears to mothers, anxieties and terrors to
children. I myself suffered throughout my childhood from
the accusation of blood guilt. Every Christian holiday was
transformed by the legend into a day of fear and sorrow for
the Jews.

But greater than the damage it did to Jews, greater even
than the destruction of Jewish lives, was the damage and
destruction it wrought upon spiritual lives.

The condition has been created that the church, on the one
hand, has preached hatred toward the Jews, has poisoned the
minds, the hearts, and the souls of its adherents with the most
horrible legends concerning them, has attributed everything
evil to the Jew, has mocked at his faith, derided his sufferings,
laughed at his tears; and, on the other hand, has wondered
why the Jew does not embrace Christianity which despises
him, why he declines a faith which robs him of his dearly
bought hopes, his reward for all the miseries he has gone
through—the Messiah, in other words—and turns him over
to his bloodiest enemies; a faith which has provided him with
the role of a Judas and given him the position of the Wandering Jew within the framework of its doctrine. From one side,
Christians have hounded the Jews, and from the other they
have sought to make him accept their faith. He has been sub-
jected to every penalty of the law, every kind of persecution
and misery; his cries unto God have been interpreted as stub-

bornness, his self-immolation for his faith has been regarded as the work of Satan. They could do anything to the Jew—they could make his life one long chain of tortures, confine him in crowded ghettos, release him to the fury of the mob, which was constantly goaded into a rage against him, restrict his rights, degrade his dignity as a man, throw him into the bonfires ignited by the monks—but his trust in God could not be broken, because it was not against the weak, tortured Jew that the sword of the church struck—oh, the weak Jew could have been overcome easily enough by the sword—but it struck instead against the impregnable armor of the destiny of eternal Israel, and therefore it had to break.

If you believe that Jesus of Nazareth is the Messiah, then you must also believe that the fact of his being born, being incarnated, so to speak, among the despised and lowly Jews instead of among the mighty, victorious Romans—a circumstance which would no doubt have been much more convenient for Christianity—was no accident, no historical caprice, but that it was God's will that the Messiah be born under these particular conditions and not under some other ones. The coming of the Messiah was something that had to be prepared: A whole line of patriarchs was necessary, all standing under the eyes of a living God, promises, prophecies, merits, election both as to suffering and deliverance—in a word, the whole heritage of the Jewish people, which the church at the beginning had accepted as the unconditional necessity for the preparation, the creation, and the appearance of the Messiah.

Because of this, the existence of the Jews was postulated as a necessary condition for the origin of Christianity and the church. But though he was flesh of their flesh, soul of their soul, had come to them and for them, the Messiah from the very beginning was endowed by the church with attributes which it was impossible and unnatural for the Jewish spirit to accept. If the Graeco-Roman individual, upon taking the new faith, killed the old self within him and was born anew, such an acceptance on the part of the Jew did not constitute a disruption but a fulfillment, a completion, an exaltation of the "old self" within him. "Think not that I am come to destroy the law, or the prophets: I am not come to destroy but to fulfil." Bound up with the Torah, which had become second nature to him, raised in blood because of his belief in one living God, the Jew correctly saw the Messiah not as the disrupter of the Mosaic Law but as one who would build upon it, not as a destroyer of the sacred principle of unity enunciated in the words "Hear, O Israel, the Lord our God is One" but as a comforter. The church, which accommodated itself to the psychology, the receptive possibilities, the habits and customs of the pagan peoples, offered the Jews a messianic idea which was entirely foreign and incomprehensible to the Jewish mind and was opposed to everything it held holy and dear. Just as there is a physical nature in man, which has developed through the law of selection, so the spiritual person has likewise a special nature which has developed through tradition, self-sacrifice, holiness, and martyrdom. And just as the physical man cannot compel his physical nature, so the spiritual man cannot force his spiritual nature. The Jew does not possess the spiritual resources to comprehend the division of the godhead into three parts. He can create "functionaries" to serve the compulsory needs of his religious development, as he actually did through the Cabala, through mysticism. Cabala created for its purposes a host of heavenly agents, angels, who were the instruments of the divine invention, and created also a symbol of the divine presence. Such ideas ran parallel to those of other faiths. But to ask the Jew to divide the unity of God was equivalent to suggesting that he should dance on thin air. The Jews possess only one God and one Messiah—"God and the Messiah"—and every other conception is alien to them.

But the church needed the Jews to bear witness to its truth. If it was impossible to win them over by means of kindness, then it was necessary to try outrage and murder as methods of compelling the Jewish spirit to violate itself.

And so the long Jewish martyrdom begins.

Christianity does not carry the sole responsibility for the Jewish tragedy. Mohammedanism did not distinguish itself any more nobly toward the Jews. Maimonides and his family had to suffer at the hands of the Mussulmen all the persecutions, tortures, agonies, and wanderings which Abarbanel suffered from the Catholic Church at the time of the expulsion of the Jews from Spain. We have only to read the letter of consolation from Maimonides to the Jews of Temen to get a small idea of what the believers in the prophet did to the Jews. There was a competitive race between church and mosque to see which could reach the goal first of forcing Jewish religious character to violate its own nature. But what have I to do with Mohammedanism? Did Mohammed pretend to be the Jewish Messiah? Is Mohammed a product of the Jewish spirit? Is Mohammed a continuation of the line of the prophets? Is Mohammed a fulfillment of the Lord's promise? Did Mohammed assure anyone at any time of anything but the sword? Was it Mohammed who preached the Sermon on the Mount? Did Mohammed create the culture and civilization of which I am part, and in the realization of which I see the greatest good fortune of humanity? Are the Mohammedans my brothers, sharing equally with me in the heritage of the patriarchs, subject to the same promises and taking part in the same privileges as myself? What have I to do with the desert tribe? The Christians are my brothers.

Chapter IV

THE SON OF GOD AND THE SON OF SATAN

WHO will dare to assert that the fact that the Jews have survived every trial of their faith is a completely naturalistic phenomenon—that it was due entirely to their own will and strength of character? He who dares to say this is either spiritually a cripple who is entirely incapable of comprehending a transcendental occurrence, or a godless cynic whose heart is a nest for the lowest passions. Go down on your knees, man, before the miracle in front of your eyes, the miracle of the preservation of Israel. If ever there has occurred in human history an event that frightens us with its incomprehensibleness and unrealizability, an event which is shrouded in a veil of profound mysticism, it is this miracle of the survival of the Jewish people.

Every living Jew is part of the miracle. The Jew as an idea, the historical Jew, is a mystic phenomenon, a Lazarus risen from the grave, because we are ignorant of the powers that have withheld him from the death and disappearance which have threatened to engulf him right down to our own time.

No historian, no philosopher can explain it satisfactorily. We can see in it only the will of God. Jews have been forced to survive, through all their sufferings, not for the sake of themselves as individuals but for the sake of the group, for the sake of the whole of which they are a part. The instinct for survival which is the chief factor in man's existence should, it seems, have compelled each individual Jew to renounce a faith which brings upon him destruction, shame, and hate, and should have forced him to accept a belief which at once opens the doors of all ghettos for him, rids him of his chains, and makes him a full-fledged member of society in good standing, without which his existence is at best a disappointing one In Poland, every Jew who changed his faith and accepted Christianity was admitted automatically into the highest aristocracy. Who dares to say that the tortured Jew in the Polish ghetto, who was a natural target for every churl, forbore to accept the aristocracy which awaited him on the other side of the ghetto wall, ready to embrace him like a young bride, simply out of willfulness or firmness of character?

If this was indeed accomplished through the strength of their own character, then the Jews are the most powerful, the most worthy, and the strongest people of the entire human race.

No, I do not ascribe these virtues to the Jews. Jews are just such weak, selfish, comfort-seeking individuals as the single members of any other people. They have survived in spite of themselves, because they were forced to do it by a superior power.

The survival of the Jews was not simply a caprice of their own or of history but a product of the fate marked out for them by God, a mission to which they are assigned, and which was kneaded into the very embryo of their existence, and forces them, against their will, to carry upon themselves the yoke of Jewry, to withstand every pain, sorrow, and persecution, to burn in every fire, to fall into every abyss—and yet to survive in spite of all. Not for themselves, not on their own behalf, but for a higher purpose, for the whole of humanity, as God had intended them.

The whole of Jewish history bears witness to it.

During the whole life span of Jewry, both before the Christian era and during it, Jews have been compelled to renounce their spiritual views, by means both fair and foul. Among the attempts stemming from good motives which were made to force them to give up their faith, I include the effort of the Greek king Antiochus Epiphanes IV and Greek society during the first half of the second century before the birth of Jesus to wean them away from their "fanatical Asiatic religion" and to incorporate them into Greek civilization.

Greek civilization in the days of the Maccabean rebellion was not one of which anybody need have been ashamed, not one to be rejected in any offhand manner. It was the civilization of the educated, cultured part of mankind at that time. Its benefits and skills, even its ethical values, not to mention its art, beauty, and literature, can stand up against those of our present civilization. In the eyes of the Greeks, the Jews were a small, fanatical tribe which had nothing to show in the realms of beauty and art. There was a very strong party among the Jews of that time which appreciated the "favor" that the Greek monarch Antiochus desired to bestow on the Jews and accepted it gratefully. The entire Jewish aristocracy in Jerusalem with the high priest at their head belonged to this party. Against the mighty Greek power, against the king's favor, against the strong Jewish aristocratic party, there stood up a handful of fanatic patriots, peasants and hill people, led by a fanatical priestly family; and they conducted first a partisan struggle and later an open war against the powerful Greek army—without any prospect of victory.

Let us pretend for a moment that the miracle of the Maccabean triumph did not come to pass, but that, as might have been expected, the Greek army together with the strong Jewish assimilationist party won out. Jerusalem is transformed into a Greek metropolis. The Jewish population at first is forced to assimilate itself with the higher Greek culture; later it follows willingly, even gratefully. Jerusalem becomes a second Alexandria, an Ephesus, a Corinth, with temples in honor of Zeus, Apollo, and Diana, adorned with all of the accustomed beauty of such places. The Jewish faith would then have disappeared—and together with it the Jewish destiny, the Jewish lot, the Jewish path of suffering. Jews would have straightened their backs. They would have become civilized people. They would have fashioned for themselves an earthly paradise instead of a heavenly one. In place of a Messiah, a redeemer who would come upon the "doubtful" path of the clouds in the sky, they would have had as their redeemer the Greek king; and with this there would have been an end to Jewish troubles. But then what would have become of the promise, made by the prophets in God's name, to bring forth the Messiah? Such a contingency would have upset the life, civilization, psychology, and conditions that were necessary for the birth of a Jesus.

For this reason, many people have learned to reckon the Christian era from the birth of the society which made possible the development of the Messianic idea.

When we consider the events in the days of the Maccabeans through the eyes of present-day Jews or Christians, we
clearly see the wonder of Jewish survival at that time. We
come to the conclusion that the stubbornness of the Jews in
resisting the Greeks and in holding on so blindly to their own
religion and traditions was not dictated by the instinct for
personal self-preservation (on the contrary, that instinct would
have urged every individual Jew along the road of Greek
assimilation) but by a higher power, which forced them to
stake their lives in order to preserve the culture which created
the basis of their existence.

We possess a tradition which instructs us that the Messiah
was born on the very day that the Holy Temple was destroyed.
We like to see in each catastrophe the birth of salvation, in
every downfall the beginning of exaltation. For this reason, we
do not accept defeat no matter how complete and annihilating
it may be. The deeper we fall, the higher we shall rise. Where
trouble is, salvation must be too, because we will not recognize
any permanent setbacks.

We are eternal. Evil may triumph for a space, but good is
everlasting.

This is the blessing which God has bestowed upon us—the
preservation of Israel.

In Rome among the first Christians, at the very outset of
the new religion, a legend sprang up by which we are told
that at the time when God sent down his son upon earth to
bring help to the people, Satan became envious of God and
he sent down his own son at the same time in order to cor-
rupt mankind and to hinder God's son from accomplishing

his mission. And so there descended upon this earth the Anti-Christ.

According to Jewish sources, Armilos, a kind of anti-Christ, will be born from a stone statue that has been impregnated by Satan. He will gather around himself all the forces of evil and lead into battle Gog and Magog against the Messiah of God. The description given of Armilos is characteristic. Among other defects, he is deaf in one ear. Whenever the truth is being told, he turns his deaf ear toward it; but let someone tell a lie and he immediately turns his good ear in that direction.

What is the power of the Anti-Christ? The power of God's son is love; the son of Satan works through hate. Great powers have been yielded to the Anti-Christ. He has access every-where. He can be found everywhere. He does not stop at any boundaries. Sometimes he can be found in a den of thieves; sometimes he appears in the heart of a mob and incites it to kill innocent human beings; at still another time he appears even in the arena of the church and drives the people to wild deeds.

Wherever the Anti-Christ appears, he sows hatred and envy among people and tears up by the roots the growth of love which Jesus of Nazareth has planted.

Anti-Semitism is one of the tried methods which the Anti-Christ uses to disrupt the work of Jesus of Nazareth. We see that anti-Semitism has not been strong enough to destroy the Jewish people. It could bring anguish and torture, sorrow and tears, burnings and murders of individuals, of whole communities, of entire countries. But if a Jewish settlement was torn up from one country, God had already planted the seeds of another in a different country. The Anti-Christ has bent all of his energies to uproot not merely a single settlement but the whole of Israel, because it is Israel that is his greatest enemy, the barrier to his success, the disrupter of his work. But against Israel he has proved too weak. His sword strikes against its armor and is shattered.

For God has surrounded Israel with a ring of fire and does not permit the destroyer to come near it. He punishes and thrashes it, but he never destroys it.

God needed the remnant of Israel. He has saved it for a mission which it is to do in the world.

But the Anti-Christ, wherever he has planted his seed of hate, has destroyed the work of Jesus, upset his garden for a time, poisoned the deeds of honest Christianity for many generations, and undermined the work of God. No matter through what channels it flows, the poison of anti-Semitism which they give out stems from but a single source, the same source: namely, from the origin of all corruption and pollution, the Anti-Christ.

"By their fruits ye shall know them.... Not everyone that saith unto me, Lord, Lord, shall enter into the kingdom of heaven; but he that doeth the will of my Father which is in heaven. Many will say to me in that day, Lord, Lord, did we not prophesy by thy name, and by thy name cast out devils, and by thy name do many mighty works? And then will I profess unto them, I never knew you: depart from me, ye that work iniquity."

About whom were these words of Jesus spoken?

From Rome, a call went out. It found an echo in the hearts of the masses, in the scattered cities of the whole of Christendom: "Come, let us go to Jerusalem and deliver the holy places from the hands of the infidels."

Companies of pious folk gather together; mixed with them are darker elements, adventurers, idlers, spoils-seekers, those who are simply thirsty for blood. Their passions are fired by the sermons of fanatical monks, priests, and clericals. Armed bands, hordes of men with knives, scythes, and hatchets stretch across the cities of Europe. And in each city that lies in their path, the Jewish population is massacred.

Infants are butchered before the eyes of their mothers; the venerable heads of rabbis bent over their studies are cracked open; synagogues are set afire; sacred scrolls are burned. A flood of flame was loosed upon Jewish settlements by the Crusades.

The Jewish community of the city of Mainz on the Rhine applies to the Bishop of Mainz Cathedral to save them. "When you give up your gold and silver and other costly things which you possess, I shall save you," is the answer. The Jews bring their gold and silver to the Bishop. The whole Jewish community, consisting at that time of a few scores of people with their rabbi in the lead, hides in the crypt of the Cathedral. The Crusaders enter the city of Mainz, thirsty for blood. They trace down the Jews to the Cathedral and surround it. The Bishop then comes to the Jews and says: "Only one road of escape remains open to you now—to renounce your faith and to accept our faith in the Christ. Otherwise, I shall hand you over to the mob that is waiting for you." The Jews embrace each other; they begin to sing verses of the Psalms: "Yea, though I walk through the valley of the shadow of death, I shall fear no evil." So as to make sure that the children do not weaken and fall away from the faith, or that mothers do not take pity on their babes and give them over into the hands of the unbelievers, the Jews themselves slaughter the children and sucklings before the whole community is delivered by the Bishop to the howling mob.

Where, at that moment, was to be found the spirit of him who had said, "Blessed are they which are persecuted for righteousness' sake: for their's is the kingdom of heaven"? With whom, I ask, was the spirit of Jesus the Messiah to be found, with the official representatives of the Christian faith—with the Bishop and the bloodthirsty mob—or with the Jews?

Through the narrow street of death in Toledo, Spain, a procession of the victims of the Inquisition is driven on its way. A group of people, living people, old and honored people, women, children, all dressed in "penance shirts" with candles in their hands. They are surrounded by hooded monks, priests of the Dominican order, who call themselves "the hounds of God." In front of them is carried the highest, holiest emblem of suffering and self-sacrifice, the mark of him who made suffering the sign of election by God. In the square the leading figures, the official representatives of the Christian church, are already seated. A fiery stake stands prepared in the center of the market place, where the monks and priests of the Dominican order are busily bustling about like the devils in hell with three-pronged pitchforks in their hands. The victims are led out and placed in the center of the platform. And when the monks set the rosin-covered wood afire, to the accompaniment of church bells, a prayer is heard coming from the victims, a song: "I shall dwell in Thy tents forever, and I shall hide myself within the sheltering places of Thy wings. Selah."

What had been their sin? The people bound up with the Pentateuch of Moses, which their fathers accepted from Mount Sinai, had observed the ceremony of Passover, taught to them by Moses in the name of God, concerning which Jesus the Messiah had borne witness: "For verily I say unto you, Till heaven and earth pass away, one jot or one tittle shall in no wise pass away from the law, till all things be accomplished."

On which side was the "Son of God" to be found, and where was to be found the son of Satan, the Anti-Christ?

With the cry "Lord, Lord," with crosses in their hands, the monks broke into Jewish synagogues and dragged after themselves the maddened masses of people. The basest instincts of the mob were aroused, while they used for their purposes the pains, the holy martyrdom, the precious blood which Jesus spilled to save the world. This blood was used to inflame and incite the dark powers, the lowest elements, to pillage, murder, rape—in fact, to turn the whole of familiar Christianity upside down.

In every country, for hundreds of years, they broke into synagogues and Jewish seminaries of learning. They dragged out books and dumped them into blazing bonfires and *autos-da-fé*. They ripped out pages, sometimes whole sections of the Holy Scriptures. Very seldom has a Hebrew book come down to us from the sixteenth and seventeenth centuries which is not disfigured by the blood-red blots of the Catholic censorship, instituted by Pope Paul IV. Entire prayers were torn out of the prayer book. Jews bewailed in lamentations and took more to heart the martyrdom of a Jewish book than of a living Jew. With whom, do you think, was the redeemer and savior to be found when they burned those writings which, according to yourselves, bear witness to his coming?

That is how the bloody thread drawn by the Anti-Christ through the whole length of Christian history reached into our own time too. Why go back to the Middle Ages and to the Inquisition? What was the state of Christian morality a day before Hitler set the world aflame?

Poland had finally regained her independence, won it through the sacrifice of young blood which the righteous nations of the world, America among them, had brought to the altar of freedom. Among the American lives lost in the First World War were not a few Jewish ones. But hardly had Poland won her freedom before she transformed her liberated territory into a prison for her own national minorities. Of the national minorities in Poland, Jews were the easiest to oppress. Poland became a hell for the Jews. Their possessions and their lives were turned over into the hands of a wild, enraged, uncontrollable youth which had been corrupted to the very marrow by empty political gabble and overblown national pride. Jewish students in the universities were persecuted; the walls of the ghetto were brought into institutions of learning. The Jewish merchant was deprived of the possibility of earning a living, by the imposition of taxes upon him which were simply confiscatory. But the full impact of the blind fury of Polish mobs, urged on by the government, fell upon the helpless, the poorest of the poor, the devoutly religious Jewish masses.

In the church, opposite the symbol of holy martyrdom, there stands a priest of the Jesuit order, which has achieved such tragic notoriety by its persecutions of the Jewish populations in every country throughout the length of Jewish history. With the subtle discourse, taught to them in their institutions of learning, not of praise or of love, which the holy name they bear demands of them, but of hatred, the priest incites the ignorant peasants and the local population against the poor, unprotected, religious Jewish population, which trusts only in the charity of God (having no other means of protection) and ekes out a woeful, poverty-stricken existence. He points to a woman who deals in soap and herring, or to a Jewish peddler who sews trousers for the peasants, and he calls them the Rothschilds, the bankers of the world, who steal the bread out of the peasant's mouth. The peasant of liberated Poland is himself poor and oppressed by the rich landlords. Instead of giving the peasants land, which the landlords have seized for themselves, Christianity puts itself in the service of the mighty and seeks to appease the hunger of the peasants with the stones they fling at the Jews.

The ignorant, bewildered peasant, who cannot orient himself with regard to his own situation, doesn't know what to do, takes in all seriousness, of course, what his spiritual adviser tells him, and throws himself with the full force of his wrath, not upon the landlords—no, the rich landowners are protected by the power of the church, which controls the conscience and can thus manipulate the behavior and point of view of the peasants—but upon the innocent, upon the poorest of the poor, who are themselves, a thousand times more so than the peasants, deprived of rights, of work, of livelihood.

In the synagogues, in the places of worship, which are sunk halfway down into the earth, with their roofs almost torn away, the Jewish population of the little town stands in prayer, nervous and trembling, fearful for the lives of themselves and their children, and they lift up their hands to heaven and cry out,

"From the depths, I called unto Thee, O Lord."

With whom was he to be found, who had said, "Blessed are they which are persecuted for righteousness' sake"? On which side, do you think, is "the son of God" and on which the son of Satan—the Anti-Christ?

More than a thousand years have passed since the German people accepted Christianity and turned to the one living God and his Messiah. Whether of their own volition or by compulsion, the Germans were a Christian people which, through its genius, produced incomparable Christian works. At the time of the greatest crisis the church has gone through, when there was great danger that the whole of Christianity might be drowned in the flood of heathenism that was pouring out of Rome, the German Reformation, created by Luther, not only saved half the world for Christianity but also exercised a tremendous influence upon the Christian community as a whole. The Reformation was the most important factor in restoring to the Catholic church its Christian conscience. And look at what has now happened to German Christianity.

Before the Reichsrat in Vienna, in the first years of this century, there stands the Viennese burgomaster as he greets a convocation of the Christian Socialist party, which he has founded. He points out that the Jews of Vienna are Austria's greatest misfortune, that the poor Galician Jews with long ear-curls are bloodsuckers upon the Austrian people, usurers and parasites, who must all be cleaned out.

A powerful boycott must be organized against the Jews. None of them should be admitted into the seats of learning, into any university. No Jew must be permitted to become a doctor or a lawyer. Jewish business must be destroyed. A really good Christian, who believes in Jesus, must not buy from a Jew, must not trade with a Jew, must avoid a Jew while he is still ten steps away. A series of exclusion laws must be passed against the Jews by which they shall be shut out of every sphere of useful activity and production, and be left only with doubtful occupations such as the brokerage business and pawnshops.

Doctor Karl Lueger preaches all this as a good Catholic in the name of Christianity—and he has organized the first Christian Socialist party which includes in its program a complete boycott against Jews, except those who are stipulated not to be Jews—that is, those who wish to be converted.

The Christian Socialist party grows up to be a strong power. It is, of course, helped, nourished, supported, and inspired by the Catholic church in Austria. Years later, there comes from the provinces to Vienna a bewildered young man. He wishes to be an artist, a painter; he takes the entrance examination of the art school of Vienna, fails, suffers from hunger, becomes embittered. The young man has boundless ambitions—a lust for world conquest dwells in his breast. He dreams of power not over the German people alone but over the entire world. A sickly imagination feeds this fantasy; the bitterness of failure strengthens his ambition. He attends a rally of the Christian Socialist party, listens to the speeches of the leaders: "The Jew is to blame for everything." The Jew is to blame that he, an Aryan, a true Austrian, is not accepted at the art school. The Jew is accepted. Did he not notice Jewish students in the school? Was it not one of them who took the examination together with him? The Jew had been accepted, while he was rejected. The Jew is to blame for everything. The Jew must become the target at which his whole hatred is aimed. The Jew is a foreigner, the Jew has foreign blood. What is he doing in a Christian society? He must be excluded. Yet . . . when he is baptized, he belongs to the Christian world, does he not? What is Christianity? It too is of Jewish origin. It too must go. It is a Jewish invention. A substitute must be found for Christianity, an *Ersatz,* into which the Jew shall be unable to smuggle himself and seem to become part of it. That is the doctrine of "race"; that is Nazism.

He who has read Hitler's *Mein Kampf* knows that Hitler's first teacher in anti-Semitism was Dr. Karl Lueger, the mayor of Vienna. Hitler recognized him as the teacher who helped him build up his hatred for the Jews, and he recognized the Christian Socialist party as the school in which he learned of Jewish domination. The Christian Socialist party, led by a Christian in the name of Christianity, was the forerunner of the Nazi party. Hitler's accomplishment was only that he drew the ultimate conclusions from the premises of Dr. Lueger. The party founded by Hitler, the National Socialist party, is an offspring of the Christian Socialist party. He appropriated its program and carried it out. He merely took out the word Christian and substituted the new conception, the new faith of Nazism.

Because the Jewish people as a whole, as an idea, as an instrument of God, is eternal, anti-Semitism has not been able and will not be able to destroy it. It is as much a part of the will of God as is Christianity, and no matter what takes place, nothing can happen to it as a group. "When thou passest through the waters, I will be with thee; and through the rivers, they shall not overflow thee; when thou walkest through the fire, thou shalt not be burned; neither shall the flame kindle upon thee"—that was said of Israel.

But anti-Semitism has, little by little, eaten away at the roots by which you are planted in God's earth, the roots through which there flow the commandments, the blessings, the moral qualities of Jesus of Nazareth. In place of the blood of the son of God, anti-Semitism has injected into your veins the blood of the son of Satan, the Anti-Christ. Anti-Semitism has poisoned the seed, has undermined the tree—and just see the fruit which it has begun to give forth.

What Hitler has done is merely the consequence, the last link in a long chain of sin and evil implanted by anti-Semitism among Christian folk. Hitler has spun a poisoned web of hatred and envy for you and involved you along with himself. He is the apostle of the Anti-Christ, driving along the same furrow which his master has made in your souls. He got you into his power, and you became accomplices to human misery. You witnessed the destroyer as he arose to eradicate a whole people from the earth. It lay in your power to stop him, and yet you were silent. You saw how the destroyer lit his fires upon Jewish business firms and dwellings, and you did not quench the flames—they spread across the national boundaries and ignited your own homes.

You tasted the bread you had helped to sow. Your eyes grew blind with the blindness of hatred, your ears were stopped with the noise of murder and violence. That is why you showed such tolerance toward the deeds of shame that Hitler carried on against the Jewish people. You might have crushed the reptile when it made its first poisonous lunge. Instead of that, you fed the viper at your breast until it was strong enough to throw itself at your neck.

And now we stand in the very midst of the bath of blood which men have made upon each other. All of our talents, all of our skills, all of our thoughts and of our genius are expended upon one thing only—the destruction and uprooting of human lives. The wings of Death's angel throw their shadow upon every house. We stand bewildered and amazed in the forest, where man used to be a wild beast. The forest is covered over with eternal darkness. It is lit only by the flames of fear, of destruction, and of death.

There is nothing left us but a single spark of a belief in God, smoldering in the heap of ashes, the ashes left by the conflagration of our spiritual estates.

Keep the flame of faith burning in your hearts, spread it, purify it—it can lead you out, you and ourselves, from the darkness and the night.

"Ask, and it shall be given you; seek, and ye shall find; knock, and it shall be opened unto you." For, in your heart, there lives the kernel of good planted by Jesus of Nazareth.

Chapter V

THE JUDAEO-CHRISTIAN IDEA

FORGIVE me, Christian, for the sharp-edged words which have fallen from my pen like drops of blood. Forgive me, Christian, that I, a stranger, a mere outsider, take the liberty of disturbing and awakening the Christian conscience within you. It is the reverence which I have for your faith, it is the love, the devotion, and the faithfulness which I feel toward the founder of your religion; it is my belief, my deep faith in the eternal, truthful religious and ethical values of the Judaeo-Christian ideal, which give me the courage and—I may permit myself to say also—the right to assume toward you the attitude of one brother talking to another.

The mystery of the messianic idea has created a religious character which is common to both Jew and Christian. It created similar religious values in both faiths; and though these faiths which flowed from the same source stood opposed to each other, yet they developed along parallel lines and built up a spiritual nature common to the believing Christian and Jew. Not only did the common heritage of the Ten Commandments, the Mosaic Law, and the hope of the prophets work in parallel fashion for both religions; even more important was the expectation of a redeemer and the whole mystery surrounding the personality of the Messiah, which acted similarly upon the character of each faith and contributed to the formation of a religious nature in both that coincides at many points.

It is the greatest mistake to believe that the messianic mystery had a small influence upon the Jewish faith. In spite of the rationalists who untiringly did their best to take from the Jewish religion its crown, to cut the wings from the divine idea, and to make it fit into the Procrustean bed of the Aristotelian *Weltanschauung,* the messianic idea overcame every stumbling block which was placed in its path.

Maimonides' rationalistic conception of the Messiah, a conception kept strictly within the framework of the natural order of things, did not gain much favor. With all due respect to the authority of Maimonides, the religious leaders rejected it, and some of them even decried it as atheism and fought against it bitterly. The Jewish people, for which the messianic ideal became the sole recompense for its faith in God, did not wish to allow its Messiah to be divested of the divine and kingly robe which the prophets and later myth-makers had woven for him. The Messiah was not only the heavenly personage whom the prophet Daniel had visioned coming with the clouds of the sky, but he was even endowed with the crown of martyrdom. The Messiah constructed by Maimonides and later rationalists of the reform epoch could not satisfy the Jewish masses' thirst for faith in salvation. The people expected a Messiah who would come upon the clouds of the sky and be accompanied by the hosts of heaven. Such a Messiah seemed reasonable to them and far more natural than the Messiah whom Maimonides draws—a Messiah who will accomplish his great mission by quite ordinary means and in accordance with the laws of nature. The natural path of the Messiah in the concept of Maimonides is more fantastically unreal than the divine road of the Messiah of Chassidism and of the Cabalists.

Even Maimonides himself made the messianic idea and the whole mystery of messianism—the resurrection of the dead—one of the chief dogmas of the Jewish faith. And similarly, too, must the reformed rabbis correct the mistake of the rationalistic founder of "Reformed Judaism." Whoever was raised in the pure spirit of Judaism, in its very pristine form—that is to say, in orthodox Jewry—knows the meaning and place which the messianic mysteries occupy in his religious life. The writer was brought up in a faith which made the Messiah the answer to all hopes and expectations and desires not only for a more just and better world but for a whole new order of the world—an order not based upon laws of an earthly nature but upon the laws of a higher nature, of a divine nature, which knows no limits, an order of the world where the visions of the prophets, of Isaiah and Ezekiel, become living realities.

The wealthy, educated Jew, perhaps, did not have to look forward to the messianic order of the world; he was able to find comforts enough in the existing order and made it, naturally, the point of departure for the messianic world; he could easily subtract a vast amount from the messianic ideal and make it fit into the rationalistic, liberal age. The poor Jew, on the other hand, could not have survived a day, with the deprivations and worries which chased after him like wolves, except for his belief in the Messiah as a means of escape, a reward for all his sufferings, all the wrongs and persecutions loaded upon him by an unjust world. The Messiah for him is the one who will answer every question and will straighten out everything which is now awry.

The messianic mystery, I should say, is responsible more than any other factor for the survival of the Jews until the present time. The mystery of the Messiah was no religious fantasy to the Jew but a reality which formed for him the ground on which he could exist, because no other ground was permitted him.

The religious Jew in his spiritual outlook is the same believer in his Messiah as the religious Christian. The mystery of the Messiah acted on both of them and created in them a single spiritual character. The religious Jew waits every minute of the day for the coming of the Messiah, as the religious Christian awaits the Second Coming—not for a righteous ruler who will install a just order in the world, or a "liberal" order, but for a mysterious personage, half-God, half-man, who was with God before he created the world; a personage who will have the power to change not only our own nature but the nature of the animals as well—the lion shall lie down with the lamb, and a child will play together with both of them; a mysterious personage who will fulfill the vision of Ezekiel—the graves will open and the earth shall give up the dead; there will take place the resurrection of the dead, for which every religious Jew says prayers three times every day.

Only for such a Messiah was it worth while to have passed through all sorrows and to spin out the thread of Israel's existence, which began to be woven in the hands of Abraham and has extended down to our own time. Only with the strength that emerges out of messianism could Jewry survive in the lime kiln which the world has lighted for it. Rob the

Jews of the messianic mystery and they must fall apart, as have so many other faiths which were built upon the sandy foundations of rationalism.

It is my firm conviction that the majority of the millions of Polish Jews whom Hitler threw into his fiery ovens while they were still alive—as they were dragging themselves to the ovens with their last ounces of strength, led by their rabbis—that these Jews saw the Messiah during their last moments as he reached out his hands to them from the tongues of flame and received their souls with mercy and pity. The messianic ideal with all of the mysteries which surround it—the resurrection of the dead, the beginning of an absolutely just order of the world—remained the final hope which they took with them from the horrible, wicked world in which they found themselves to that other, better world into which they entered across the thresholds of the lime kilns Hitler had prepared for them.

The hope for the messianic ideal not only was the consolation of those who went to their death but has remained the sole hope of that last remnant of Israel in which the word of the Bible has been left alive—"one of a thousand and two from a family."

I cannot see with what moral powers the remnant of Israel will begin anew its life upon an earth which has split open and swallowed the greatest number of them, if it is not to be with the strength of the hope which is given by the messianic idea.

And why the Jews alone?

The whole world finds itself more or less in the same situation as Israel—if not in a physical then in a spiritual sense.

It is not merely Hitler and his Nazis who are to be blamed for what took place in Germany; we are all accomplices in the German wickedness. The moral status of our generation between the wars had created the atmosphere that made the misdeeds of Germany possible. If a human being can descend to the point of skinning another human being with the purpose of making a lamp shade of the skin, what will stay him from using the stripped corpse for nourishment? The whole human race had fallen from its God-chosen heights to the state of a beast.

But who are those who will build the new world? What is their moral position? What powers will be working within them? From what source will they gather the moral strength which must surge up within the people if our new society is to be built upon the foundation of a more equitable order of the world?

It cannot be claimed that they will draw these moral powers from the events of the war or from the state of the world before the war, from a moral condition which made it possible to bring mankind to the brink of the greatest catastrophe and the greatest danger to the existence of our established morality.

We often hear talk that the war puts Christian morality in danger and that we stand at the end of the Christian epoch.

Yes, I believe this too—that is to say, I believe it if our enemies, both those within and those without, should, may God forbid it, retain their satanic beliefs after the war . . . if the forces of darkness emerge uncowed from the struggle, or smuggle themselves into our society and become an important factor after they have been vanquished on the field of battle. They have wiped out the teachings, the morality, and the mystery of Christianity. They have put it to shame and laughed at it and labeled it an Asiatic weakness; on the other hand, in their own philosophy they have made cardinal principles of everything that Jesus and his apostles rejected and overcame. Instead of Christian pity, mercy, and love, which Jesus inculcated, the leading themes of their outlook became pagan cruelty, the power of the naked fist, and the strength of force that was purely physical. Particularly have the "Christians" among them sinned a thousand times more grievously and made themselves a thousandfold greater danger to the existence of the Christian religion than the idol-worshiping Nazi fascists.

We know exactly where we stand with the pagan fascists of Hitler's school. They engaged in open war against us— as did we against them. The lines are sharply drawn. But what is to be done with a type of fascism which utilizes the sacred personage of the founder of the Christian religion as a weapon to bring torture and anguish upon innocent people, to implant enmity and race hatred in the hearts of its followers? What is to be done with a neo-Catholic fascism, which has arisen in Spain and in our own hemisphere, and which puts up the flag of the church over the temples of Moloch? If the Argentine fascists and their like are still regarded as Christians, then the religion has descended once more to the state of paganism in which Paul found it in Corinth and Ephesus, before he won these cities for Christianity.

On the other hand, there are a number of conflicting signs that never since the days of Constantine, when the church became militant, did Christianity attain to such a height and come so near to fulfilling the commandments of Jesus—both in word and in deed—as it has in our own time. It may be claimed without exaggeration that in some respects Christianity has risen in the present time to the unsurpassed height which it reached during the first three hundred years of the spread of the new religion. With nearly the same willingness to pay the highest price in self-sacrifice, Christians in our day have sanctified the name of their faith even as their ancestors did long ago. We must remember the millions of Christian soldiers who have given their lives to restore the world to the civilization founded on the Judaeo-Christian teachings.

I wish to bring as an instance of Christian conduct in our days the behavior of Christians of all sects and creeds toward the suffering Jews. I bring this instance because in their behavior toward the Jews we have always had an index of the amount of truly Christian spirit that existed among believers. The attitude toward the Jews is the barometer which has registered how much Christian spirit there is among Christians.

Quite aside from the fact that of all international movements, including the socialist, Christian faiths of all creeds have best withstood the crucial test of resistance against Hitlerite paganism, Christianity also distinguished itself, in the particular of rescuing Jewish children, by the highest degree of self-sacrifice. It may be stated without exaggeration that almost the entire remnant of Israel which was found in the liberated countries—no matter how small its number—has the Christians to thank for its preservation, Christians who, by performing this action, placed their own lives in danger. By this great act of saving a segment of Jewry, more especially the children, all creeds of the Christian faith, beginning with the Pope's and extending to that of the idealistic Quakers, have shown themselves to be worthy before the God of Israel and his Messiah—and before world history. There were times when the Pope supported within the narrow bounds of the Vatican over five thousand Jewish souls who had saved themselves from destruction. Aside from the small sum which the Joint Distribution Committee was able to send through the representative of the Vatican in America, a sum which could cover the expenses of only a small number of refugees, the Vatican out of its own funds fed, clothed, and housed five thousand souls until they eventually achieved their liberation through the efforts of the Allied powers. The Vatican did this in imminent danger of being stormed by Hitlerite bandits, as the Gestapo openly threatened the Holy Father.

Apart from the five thousand who were rescued, Italian Catholics are responsible for saving thousands upon thousands of Jewish families who found aid and comfort in churches, monasteries, and in private Christian homes.

In France, under the greatest risk to themselves, Christians rescued over fifty thousand Jewish children from death. Christian institutions such as cloisters and churches, and a host of private persons, undertook to conceal the Jewish children who had been smuggled out of Paris by a Jewish underground committee. The same thing occurred in Belgium and Holland. The Jews who saved themselves in these countries were spared only through the fact that they found hiding places in Christian homes. Even in Poland and other backward lands the conscience of the common Christian awakened to its duty. Ignorant Polish peasants risked their lives and took Jewish children into their homes. Thousands of Jewish souls were rescued in Poland, in Galicia, and even in Rumania, through the intervention of Christian institutions and of private people. The same picture can be seen everywhere. The Christian conscience, awakened to its duties, achieved the miracle which the same self-sacrifice had accomplished when the first Christians risked their lives for their faith; the same heroic qualities were exhibited in our own time in the rescue of tens of thousands of Jews from the destroyer.

Note the difference in attitude toward us, in the hour of our greatest trial, between the Christian believers and the Mohammedans. Lulled by the opinion often expressed by learned Jews who lived in Mohammedan lands, that the Mohammedan religion is nearer to us, through the monotheistic principle which it embraces, than Christianity, many Jews maintain to this day that our people may find a more sympathetic understanding in Mohammedan countries than in Christian lands, and that the Mohammedan is nearer to us because of his Semitic origin. They have entirely forgotten the fact that the lack of the messianic principle in the Mohammedan makes him an incomprehensible stranger to us.

All Christian neutral nations, with the exception of fascist Spain, showed a deep humanity, a sympathetic pity, and an understanding for our sufferings which the messianic idea had built up within them.

Switzerland accepted thousands upon thousands of refugees and supports them to this day. The Swiss government has spent many hundreds of millions of francs to help the needy. Especially noteworthy is the sheltering of children by the Swiss Christian population and their rescue from certain death.

The Swedish organizations of the Red Cross and of the Salvation Army have accomplished wonders. They entered into the lion's jaws and carried on God's work there. They extended help by every means in their power to the victims in the occupied countries, where these found themselves in the shadow of death. The high point of distinction was reached in Hungary, where they rescued thousands and thousands of victims of hunger and cold—not to mention the fact that Sweden opened wide her frontiers and freely invited, in the very face of the Nazi menace, all Jews from Norway and Finland who were able to save themselves, and supports them to this very day.

As against this Christian action on the part of neutral Christian countries, Turkey, which found itself in a much more formidable position against Germany than did the Christian neutrals, sealed her frontiers tightly against Rumanian-Jewish refugees who, fearful for their lives, tried to steal across the border. She simply sent them back—in many cases turning them into the hands of the Nazi devils. Perhaps isolated acts of human kindness by individual Mohammedans occurred in this hour of need, but we heard nothing of such organized charity as was tendered by the Christians. Not only were those Jews whom Turkey was afraid of being left to care for not allowed to cross her frontier, but even Jews with means, who possessed visas to emigrate to Palestine, were forbidden by her—like Amalek of old—to cross the borders which were the only doors of rescue for victims hounded by the Nazis. Only much later, after the direct intervention of President Roosevelt, did the Turkish government make the necessary concession and allow seven or eight Jews with visas for Palestine to cross her borders each day—at a time when tens of thousands were knocking at her doors seeking escape from certain death and annihilation. By keeping back the stream of refugees from her borders, Turkey necessarily delivered them into the hands of their destroyers.

And our Semitic brethren in Palestine—how have they behaved toward us? When Rommel together with his barbarous hordes of Nazis stood at the gates of Alexandria and the danger was great that they might soil the Holy Land with their unclean fingers, the Arabs in Palestine came out of their burrows and openly began to sharpen their knives in preparation for the cutting of Jewish throats as soon as the Germans should have crossed the borders. They parceled out Jewish lands among themselves ahead of time—those lands which had been recovered by the Jews with the expenditure of so much sweat and toil, and which the Arab representative in Berlin, according to the terms of an agreement with Hitler, was to get in return for Arab aid to the Nazis. Impudently these Arabs appeared in Jewish settlements and marked with chalk the houses, stalls, gardens, and factories which they had betimes distributed among themselves. They also took upon themselves prospectively a little bit of the work of Hitler's bandits—to slaughter Jewish fathers, mothers, children, and to divide up the daughters among their own harems.

They frankly sharpened their knives for Jewish throats, and as a reward for their loyal attitude to the enemy who was knocking on the doors of the Holy Land, Bible-loving and Christian England presented them with the gift of the "White Paper." With stiff-necked British consistency, the Minister of Colonies in the Palestine administration allowed ships to sink that were carrying hundreds of human lives. After stormy experiences on the sea and after saving themselves from a thousand dangers, Jewish refugees finally reached the shores of Palestine. But the borders were sealed with seven seals against those who had fled before death and annihilation. On the other hand, England opened wide the doors of the Holy Land to the Arabs of neighboring countries who, not being bound by Jewish-Christian morality, can breed children from the scores of wives whom they possess, and so become the majority in the land where Jewish effort, Jewish money, and Jewish idealism have created economic and cultural conditions which the Arabs find nowhere among themselves. Bible-loving and Christian England has reserved Palestine, the land that has produced the highest moral good for humanity, the Jewish-Christian ideal, for the Mohammedan faith, thereby forgetting that the return of the Jews to Palestine is a condition for the coming of the Messiah set by both Jewish and Christian prophets. *not so fast*

I know of no time in the history of both faiths when Jewish-Christian understanding and *rapprochement* became the conscious desire of the leading spiritual powers and the broad masses of both factions more than it has at present. In the minds of the greatest number of Jews, especially among ourselves in America, a revolutionary change of opinion has taken place about the personage who is the symbol of the Christian faiths, as it has, too, about the Christian faiths themselves. The same thing may be said of a great number of representatives of the Christian religion, because never before have so many Christian elements shown such willingness to understand and to investigate the nature of Jewry, and to give ear sympathetically to Jewish needs.

In time of stress we have both found ourselves. For Hitler

and his hordes of fascists did not lift their hands against the Jews alone but against the very root from which Christianity springs, against the Jewish-Christian ideal, which contains in it the only cure for an ailing world.

It is my profound belief that only the Jewish-Christian idea contains in itself the possibility of salvation for our tortured world. The Jewish-Christian idea makes us equal partners in your Christian ideal, just as it make you equal partners in our Jewish one, in spite of the fact that we belong to separate faiths. For if faith in the Messiah makes you partners to the promise and—through that—inheritors of the legacy for those springing from Abraham, Isaac, and Jacob, then our belief in a single God and in the truthfulness of the prophecies makes us equal partners in the civilization, the fruit and the blessings, which realization of the promise has brought to humanity— even though we rejected the dogma which our religious nature did not permit us to accept. The substantial fact that you and we believe in the same God of Israel, that both of us have taken upon ourselves the yoke of heaven, that we believe in salvation, in redemption, in the promise, that we await the redeemer, the Messiah, each day, each hour, and each minute, that we expect him to come upon the clouds of the sky, that we believe the world cannot become perfect without the redeemer—all this has given us, it might be said, a common faith, a common psychology, and common character traits. But the real essence of the matter is that our religions have imposed upon us the same duties, the Ten Commandments which we hold in common, and the obligations to perform good deeds and acts of benevolence toward our neighbors. The fear of God which we have in common has implanted in us the fear of sin, and our love of God a love of mankind. Our hope for a life after death has made us partners in a moral possession which is the sole consolation of our life; the expectation of the Messiah is our only reward. All of this together has created our civilization, which is founded upon the common element of the Jewish-Christian idea.

We are equal partners in our common heritage.

The messianic faith is based on the conception that our order of things, our world, is not perfect and waits for a savior to redeem it. This conception has created in the souls of the believers in a Messiah a seeking, a longing, a sense of expectation which has given them a tragic quality and an everlasting restlessness. This characteristic is common only to believers in a messianic religion and is contrary to the conception of an aesthetic order such as Buddhism or Mohammedanism.

This searching after salvation, the hopeful expectation of a Redeemer, has created the prophets, the Psalms, the Epistles of Paul, the ethics and mystic teachings of the rabbis, and of St. Augustine and St. Francis, the moving prayers of the Hebrew prayer book, the hymns of the Christian churches, and the different creeds of Christianity. In fact, the evolution of all our cultural achievement was inspired by the belief in the Messiah. The dynamic force of our faith is responsible for the dynamic force of our civilization.

Judaism in one form or another has come to rule the world because it contained within itself the potentiality of a world ideal imparted to it by divine inspiration. If the given form was too narrowly nationalistic to embrace the rest of the world, it gave rise to a new power—grown out of the strength that is enfolded in the very essence of its embryonic growth—and assumed the form which was necessary to suit the Graeco-Roman man. But beneath the new clothes, Judaism worked along its original lines, destroyed the old pagan man and created a new nature within him, gave birth to a new conscience and molded the civilization which goes by the name of Christian. Good or bad, it is our civilization; the other is the one which Hitler wishes to create.

In this civilization, we Jews have an equal part. We are partners to it because it grew out of the foundation we laid, and its pure nature is the nature of the Jews; its virtues are those which our Bible, our prophets, and our Psalms have set as an example. Its highest ethical strivings were created through the messianic ideal.

It took us a long time to recognize this, to understand it clearly. The smoke from the *autos-da-fé* which the Inquisition lighted hid the truth from us as with a veil. Rivers of blood placed barriers between us; but in the new sun which America created in the sky of faith, we saw the light. Our readiness for mutual recognition, the love and respect which we have for each other, are beginning to cover over the bloody abyss that has separated us. Nourished upon the same religious substances, showered with the same blessings, and impelled by the same longing for God and his divine justice, a single nature is being produced within us, the nature of the Jewish-Christian man.

When Hitler came to power, he tried with all his might to uproot this nature from mankind and to implant a different one instead—the nature of the old beast-man. He accomplished this in his own country, among his own people, by raising a whole generation of Germans in his spirit. He forced upon the German the skin of an animal in the forest, he tore up by the root all the blessings and the whole great sum of spiritual values which faith in the Jewish-Christian ideal had created in the soul of European man, and he instilled into him the instincts of a beast by forced upbringing, by agitation and propaganda, and by awakening within him the lust to pillage, steal, and murder. He spread his influence over many peoples, scattered his idols over many lands, sowed his seed of evil in many hearts, until the evil matured and he was able to cut the full harvest of the seeds he had planted. The result was the catastrophe which he brought upon us, the fire which he turned upon our homes, our cities, our countries, our whole world.

There is no place in the world for two rival powers, for both God and the devil. One must make way for the other—and we are committed in this war to the task of clearing out the devil in order to make room for the dominion of God.

And what is the dominion of God?

The dominion of God consists of the commandments he has given us through his chosen prophets—both of the Old and the New Testaments. The will of God is expressed through Christ and the Sermon on the Mount. These teachings created our civilization, which we call the civilization of the Jewish-Christian idea. We live and die for this civilization, because it is the only one which contains the possibility of salvation for our life at present and a hope for life after death in the expectation of the resurrection of the dead.

I can see no hope for our unhappy world save that which

lies in the renewal of the moral and spiritual estates which our common ideal of faith has created—in our strengthening hold upon those possessions and in our turning to them with hearts full of faith, in fear of God, in love for him, and in love for his creation—Man.

That is the road for our tortured world. That is the reward which we can hold out to our children for their efforts, when they return, bloody, from the long night of fear and anxiety. It is the hope we can give to those who have paid the highest price in the war. It is the means of rescue we can throw to our enemy, not to slay the sinner but to slay sin itself.

We must all together help each other in finding the way back to God. No one among us can do it alone. There is no longer a righteous island within a sea of sin. Sin and crime, wherever they show themselves, spread like a disease and plague the whole world. The world is becoming more shrunken each day with the development of new means of communication. We are dependent not only upon how our neighbor is conducting himself, the neighbor who lives next door to ourselves, but upon the neighbor in the Japanese islands or the German plague-land. We are all inhabitants of the same world, and the world must belong to God or to the devil. No division of authority exists any longer, because we all share in a single fate.

America, which is the healthiest country in a sick world, must take upon itself the mission of renewing the hopes of mankind—America, which was established with the purpose that she might understand all men. It is upon America, young and strong in her faith, that the mission has been placed of renewing the Jewish-Christian ideal as the only means of salvation for a world in flames. And that is the gift America will bring to the faith in God.

In our own time, humanity has been brought to the level of the beasts. The dignity of the human being, that sacred position bestowed on him by the Judaeo-Christian religion, can be restored only by acceptance and submission to its teachings.